The Foreign Policies of West European Socialist Parties

edited by

Werner J. Feld

The Praeger Special Studies program, through a selective worldwide distribution network, makes available to the academic, government, and business communities significant and timely research in U.S. and international economic, social, and political issues.

The Foreign Policies of West European Socialist Parties

Praeger Publishers New York London

Library of Congress Cataloging in Publication Data

Main entry under title:

The Foreign policies of West European socialist parties.

(Praeger special studies in international politics and government)
Includes bibliographical references.
1. Political parties—Europe. 2. Socialist parties.
3. Europe—Foreign relations. I. Feld, Werner J.
JN94.A979F67 1978 329.9'4 77-83485
ISBN 0-03-039381-7

Published in the United States of America in 1978
by Praeger Publishers,
A Division of Holt, Rinehart and Winston, CBS, Inc.

89 038 987654321

Printed in the United States of America

PREFACE

In times of economic malaise and political change new political forces are likely to arise and existing political constellations may be altered. In Western Europe, the French socialists have emerged during the last few years as a potent force in France; in Lisbon the socialist party controls the government since Portugal's return to democracy; and in Spain's new democratic system the socialists are certain to play a major role. On the other hand, the British Labour Party and the German Social Democrats (SPD) have been losing strength and their current control of government has become shaky.

This book focuses on the changing fortunes of selected socialist parties in Western Europe with special emphasis on the implications for the foreign policies of the countries involved. The contributors to this book are experts in their fields; they seek to analyze the foreign policy attitudes of the respective parties and assess their impact on international politics, especially as far as the European Community, NATO, and the relations with Eastern Europe are concerned.

It is always difficult to assemble into a book the manuscripts of different authors located in various parts of America and Western Europe. But this task was even more difficult because it was considered essential to bring out this book quickly while the political changes were still in process. That this task was accomplished successfully is due mainly to the executive ability and devotion of Janet Davis, who effectively coordinated matters in New Orleans while I was part of the time in Berlin serving as Visiting Professor at the Free University. My deepest gratitude goes to her for handling so well this difficult transatlantic enterprise and expertly typing the manuscript. My thanks go also to the contributors to this volume for their willing response to my request to furnish their manuscripts and revisions as quickly as possible.

CONTENTS

	Page
PREFACE	v
LIST OF TABLES AND FIGURES	ix
LIST OF ACRONYMS	x
Chapter	
1. INTRODUCTION Werner J. Feld	1
Fluctuations in Strength	1
Purpose and Scope of the Book	3
Eurosocialism and Eurocommunism	4
A New Departure or Tactical Moves?	5
National Patterns of Socialist Party Involvement	7
Notes	8
2. THE LABOUR PARTY AND BRITISH FOREIGN POLICY John Roper	9
3. THE SOCIAL DEMOCRATIC PARTY AND WEST GERMAN FOREIGN POLICY: CONTINUITY AND CHANGE Charles R. Foster	17
Policy Trends Toward the West	20
Policy Toward the East	22
Notes	25
4. SOCIALIST PARTIES IN SWEDEN: FOREIGN POLICY AND NEUTRALITY Nils Andrén	27
The Predominant Role of the Social Democrats	27
Which Are the Socialist Parties?	29
The Social Democrats Between Left and Center: Restrictions and Possibilities	32
On Sociological Constraints	33
How European?	37
Notes	43

Chapter Page

5. SOCIALIST PARTIES IN NORWAY AND THEIR FOREIGN POLICY POSITIONS 44
Martin Saeter

Introduction 44
Some General Remarks 44
The Relevance of the Theme 45
Party Preferences Among Norwegian Voters 46
Party Titles and Abbreviations 46
The Norwegian Labour Party (Det norske Arbeiderparti-DNA) 48
Ideology 51
NATO and Europe 54
The Socialist Left Party (Sosialistisk Venstreparti-SV) 56
The Communist Party of Norway (NKP) 61
Conclusion 65
Notes 66

6. THE FRENCH SOCIALIST PARTY AND WESTERN RELATIONS 68
Jacques Huntzinger

The Triple Origins of the Socialist Party 69
The Characteristics of the Socialist Party 70
The Three Languages of the Foreign Policy of the Socialist Party 72
Eurosocialism 73
The EEC (European Economic Community) 77
Atlantic Relations 80
Recent Changes in French-American Relations 81
Notes 82

7. SOCIALIST PARTIES AND ITALIAN FOREIGN POLICY: REBUILDING A NEW POLITICAL BASE? 83
Fulvio Attina

The Neutralist "Conviction" (1947–48) 84
Atlanticism and Anti-Atlanticism (1949–55) 86
The EEC (1956–57) 89
Detente and Italy's International Position (1958–61) 89
Acceptance of NATO (1961–62) 91
The First Period of the Center-Left: European Choices, Equilibrium, and Anti-de Gaullism (1963–66) 92

Chapter Page

Unification: Persistence and Gradualism of Detente, Erosion of the Blocs (1967-69) 94
The Crisis of the Center-Left: Old Discrepancies and New Problems (1970-73) 96
The Eurostrategy 98
Notes 100

8. THE PORTUGUESE SOCIALISTS: RESTRUCTURING PORTUGUESE FOREIGN POLICY 102
Thomas C. Bruneau

Notes 119

9. SOCIALISM AND WESTERN EUROPE: THE PAST 122
George Windell

Notes 136

10. SOCIALIST TRANSNATIONAL COOPERATION AND THE FUTURE 141
Werner J. Feld

The Socialist International 141
The Federation of Socialist Parties of the EC 143
The Socialist Party Group in the European Parliament 144
Influential Variables for Socialist Party Policy Formation 145
Projections for the Future 147
Notes 149

ABOUT THE EDITOR AND CONTRIBUTORS 150

LIST OF TABLES AND FIGURES

Table		Page
3.1	Bundestag Election Results	19
4.1	Relative Significance of the Labor (Worker) Vote, 1956-73	30
4.2	Electoral Profile of Swedish Voters	30
4.3	Changes in Swedish Occupational Structure, 1950-70	33
4.4	Trade Unionism Membership, 1957 and 1974	34
4.5	Stoppages of Work	36
4.6	Sweden's Trade with EEC and EFTA, 1960-75	39
5.1	Stated Party Preferences of Norwegian Voters	47
5.2	Attitudes toward Membership in NATO and EC by Party Affiliation	50

Figure		Page
4.1	Party Development in Sweden since 1944	28
4.2	The Swedish Social Democratic Labour Party Organization	35

LIST OF ACRONYMS

AIK	Workers' Information Committee (Norway)
AKP (M–L)	Workers' Communist Party, Marxist-Leninist (Norway)
ASW	antisubmarine warfare
BAOR	British Army of the Rhine
CDU/CSU	Christian Democratic Party (Germany)
CERES	Comite d'Etudes Regionales Economiques et Sociales
CGT	Confederation General du Travail (France)
COMECON	Council for Mutual Economic Assistance
COMISCO	Committee of the International Socialist Conferences
CPSU	Communist Party Soviet Union
CSCE	Conference on Security and Cooperation in Europe
DNA	Norwegian Labor Party
EDC	European Defense Community
EC	European Community
ECSC	European Coal and Steel Community
EEC	European Economic Community
EFTA	European Free Trade Association
EP	European Parliament
ERP	European Recovery Program
FDP	Free Democrats (German Liberal Party)
FRG	Federal Republic of Germany
GDR	German Democratic Republic
IEA	International Energy Agency
IMF	International Monetary Fund
JSN	Junta of National Salvation (Portugal)
JUSO	Young Socialists (Germany)
KPÖ	Austrian Communist Party
LO	Landsorganisjonen (Norway)
MBFR	Mutual and Balanced Reduction of Forces
MFA	Armed Forces Movement (Portugal)
MRCA	Multirole Combat Aircraft
NATO	North Atlantic Treaty Organization
NGO	nongovernmental organization
NKP	Communist Party of Norway
OECD	Organization for Economic Cooperation and Development
OEEC	Organization for European Economic Cooperation

OMISCO	International Socialist Conference
ÖVP	Austrian People's Party
PCF	French Communist Party
PCI	Italian Communist Party
PCP	Communist Party of Portugal
PLO	Palestine Liberation Organization
PSB	Benelux Socialist Party
PSDI	Social Democratic Party (Italy)
PSF	Parti Socialiste Française
PSI	Italian Socialist Party
PSIUP	Italian Socialist Party of Proletarian Italy
PSLI	Social Democratic Party (Italy)
PSOE	Spanish Socialist Party
PSP	Socialist Party of Portugal
PSU	United Socialist Party
SF	Socialist People's Party (Norway)
SFIO	Section Française de l'Internationale Ouvriere
SPD	Social Democratic Party (Germany)
SPÖ	Austrian Socialist Party
SV	Socialist Left Party (Norway)
WEU	Western European Union

The Foreign Policies of West European Socialist Parties

CHAPTER

1

INTRODUCTION

Werner J. Feld

The socialist parties in Western Europe do not constitute a homogeneous group. Their philosophical tendencies, organizations, particular goals, and strategies differ. On the one side we see the more pragmatic aproaches of the West German Social Democratic Party (SPD) and the British Labour Party; on the other we witness the more ideology-oriented parties such as the *Parti socialiste* of France (PSF) transformed in 1971 from the former SFIO. Overall, these parties represent the largest West European political force with more than 5 million members and more than 50 million voters. Despite some losses in the Swedish and West German elections in the fall of 1976, socialist parties control or participate in the majority of the governments in Western Europe.

FLUCTUATIONS IN STRENGTH

Of course, the electoral fortunes of individual socialist parties rise and fall over time. The losses at the polls suffered by the SPD in the fall of 1976 have been followed by significant losses in subsequent municipal and state (*Laender*) elections that have led to shifts in governmental control from the SPD and the FDP (Liberals) to the Christian Democrats (CDU/CSU). Scandals within the ranks of the SPD leadership may portend further losses at the ballot box in the future and the possibility of a new government in the Federal Republic in 1978 without the SPD.

In Great Britain the Labour Party also suffered defeats in a number of by-elections where normally safe Labour seats fell to the Conservatives. As a consequence, Prime Minister James Callaghan has been forced to rely on an alliance with the small Liberal Party for the survival of his government. In May 1977 the Labour Party suffered an additional, very severe setback when in local elections it lost 119 seats on municipal councils across the country and had to give up control of major large urban and industrial districts.[1]

The minority government of Socialist Party leader Mario Soares in Portugal also had its difficulties. Although the Socialists remain the strongest party in Portugal with 35 percent of the vote in the April 1976 elections and 40 percent of the seats in Parliament, the Communist Party made a surprising comeback in December of that year when, during municipal elections, it increased its following from 8 to 18 percent of total votes cast. However, the Socialists continue their leading position among Portugal's parties.

Within the party Soares also encounters problems through factionalism and especially attacks against his policies from militant, well-organized leftists. From the Right, outside his party, he is being blamed for not accepting the middle-of-the-road Social Democrats into his government which would give him a broader base for policy development. All this means that Soares' hold on governmental control may be tenuous in the future and his party cannot afford to sit complacently on its laurels.

In France the story is different: the Socialists have made remarkable progress since 1969. During that year their presidential candidate, Gaston Defferre, won only 5 percent of the total votes cast. But during the early 1970s, François Mitterand built a solid front with the Communists by signing a Common Program and thereby bringing the Communists out of the political ghetto to which they had been consigned since the late 1940s. Interestingly, this alliance so far seems to have benefitted the Socialists more than the Communists. Indeed, the "new" Parti Socialiste has increased its strength at every election. It may well be that many French voters have abandoned their traditional splinter parties in order to vote Socialist and increase that party's strength more than that of the Communists. The latter, however, have done well also as demonstrated by the French municipal elections in March 1977. Although the Socialists improve their positions more than their Communist partners, many French communities now have Communist mayors and councillors.

Public-opinion polls taken after the municipal elections appear to suggest that the common front of the Left could have polled as much as 56 percent if parliamentary elections had taken place then.[2] The Socialists might have had between 30 and 35 percent of the vote and thus could be able to dominate the Communists. If such a distribution of the vote were the outcome of the 1978 parliamentary elections in France, the impact on French foreign relations could be dramatic. Policies toward the Atlantic Community, the European Community, and relations with the Communist world could undergo severe change.

PURPOSE AND SCOPE OF THE BOOK

To assess what the foreign policy changes might be in France as well as in some other countries where the socialists are currently in the opposition, and to analyze the foreign policies of countries where socialist parties are presently in control of government, is the main purpose of this book. Such analyses and assessments are not only useful for the practitioner in international relations, who must always be prepared to anticipate foreign policy changes under a variety of circumstances, but they may also make a contribution to scholarly knowledge and be of interest to the informed layman.

This book does not cover all the socialist parties of Western Europe. Since the focus is on foreign policy positions of these parties, we have confined ourselves to those countries whose external policies are likely to have a significant impact on international politics, because of either their size or location. For this reason, the countries selected are Great Britain and Germany in the central sector of Europe; France, Italy, and Portugal in the southern tier; and Norway and Sweden in the northern tier. Portugal is, of course, not only interesting because of its strategic location, but also in view of its rather recent shift from an authoritarian to a democratic political system. For that reason, the inclusion of Spain might have been instructive, where 156(!) parties competed during the June 15 elections for 350 seats in the House of Representatives and 207 seats in the Senate.[3] Of the two socialist parties offering candidates, the Socialist Workers' Party under the leadership of Felipe Gonzales emerged as the stronger, with the Popular Socialist Party not too far behind. But since the democratic evolution in Spain is too recent to permit a detailed analysis of the foreign policy attitudes of Spanish socialist party groupings and offer projections for the future, we did not include a chapter on these organizations.

The book begins with a study by John Roper, Labour MP and former professor, who examines the problems faced by the British Labour Party and its influence on foreign policy making. This is followed by a chapter on the SPD written by a long-time student of German politics, Charles R. Foster of the Atlantic Council of the United States. Professor Jacques Huntzinger of the University of Rennes, in turn, spotlights the changes that have been taking place in the French Socialist Party including its recent electoral successes and its relationship with the Communist Party. The latter also is a major theme in the analysis presented by Professor Fulvio Attina of the University of Florence on the changing fortunes and policies of the Italian Socialist Party. The Portuguese Socialist Party and its foreign policy attitudes are examined by Professor Thomas Bruneau of McGill University in Montreal.

Proceeding to the northern tier, Professor Martin Saeter of the Norwegian Institute of International Relations discusses not only the ruling Norwegian Labour Party and its foreign policies, but its interactions with smaller socialist splinter parties and the Communist Party. Finally, Nils Andrén of Stockholm analyzes the Swedish socialists and their attitudes toward foreign policy and Euro-American relations in the light of traditional Swedish neutrality. A summation and conclusions highlighting the past and speculating on the future, written by Professors Werner J. Feld and George Windell (both of the University of New Orleans) conclude the book.

EUROSOCIALISM AND EUROCOMMUNISM

During the last few years Eurosocialism has become a programmatic effort of the West European socialist parties that has implications for their foreign policy positions not only regarding European unification, but also NATO and the relations with Eastern Europe.

The formal basis for Eurosocialism stems from the establishment of the Confederation of Social Democratic Parties of the European Community in 1974. Details of the program and objectives of Eurosocialism have been discussed in many conferences of the West European socialist parties, but since the ideological approaches and strategies of the individual parties differ considerably, agreement has only been possible on the lowest common denominator. As early as 1971 the Dutch Socialist Party championed the immediate establishment of a European Socialist Party, but most other socialist leadership groups have insisted on national party autonomy.[4] The reasons are easy to understand. While the general goals of all socialist parties are the reduction of inequalities in income and wealth, the lowering of class barriers, and the direction and control of the economy by the "people" and for their maximum benefit, the approaches differ. Some parties such as the SPD, the Labour Party, and the Swedish socialists are promoting gradual social reforms, while others such as the French PS have stronger Marxist orientations and advocate more drastic, and under certain circumstances, revolutionary changes in the structure of society.

There are also more specific differences in various party platforms. For example, the German right of codetermination of workers in enterprises where they are employed has been a foremost goal and accomplishment of the SPD, but codetermination has been frowned upon by the Italian socialists. The extent of nationalization of private enterprises varies among the socialist parties and so does the degree of instituting a planned economy. All these disparities play a role in conceptualizing a unified Europe although basic agreement exists that the strong orientation toward free enterprise and the lack of accountability of the European Community (EC) institutions toward the people living in the member states must be changed to reflect social democratic tenets in a broad sense.[5] No doubt, the direct elections for the European Parliament, scheduled for May 1978 but not unlikely to be postponed by a year or more, will test the willingness of the EC socialist parties to arrive at a consensus for a uniform party platform that will offer more definitive insights into the nature of Eurosocialism.

A major stumbling bloc in the definition of Eurosocialism is the relationship of socialist parties to the Communists. Whereas the French PS has formed a highly successful common program with the French Communist Party, the SPD refuses any common action with Communists. Indeed, for the sake of credibility it could not afford to ally itself with parties that are in coalition with Communists. In this connection it is interesting to note that traditionally the socialist parties are strong and the communist parties weak in those countries where a single or a dominant trade union organization has been in existence for several decades. Examples for such a situation are Germany, Great Britain, Austria, and the Scandinavian countries. On the other hand, where the trade union movement is fragmented, the strongest union is normally closely affiliated with the communist party. The result then is likely to be a weak socialist party as is the case in Italy now and has been until fairly recently in France.

A NEW DEPARTURE OR TACTICAL MOVES?

It was the Italian Communist Party (PCI) that, under the leadership of Enrico Berlinguer, developed the concepts of Eurocommunism. They are 1) respect for democratic methods including majority rule and acceptance of and compliance with the results of periodic free elections; 2) basic recognition of the need for a free market economy and no insistence on complete nationalization of private enterprise, but extensive state planning is considered necessary; 3) strong support for the European Community and the direct elections to the European Parliament, but the Community must be "democratized"; and 4) continued membership in NATO. Obviously, these concepts are quite similar to those of the socialists, and they have now been accepted also by the French Communist Party (PCF). Its leader, Georges Marchais, much more the typical Communist party secretary-general than the elegant and sophisticated Berlinguer, made the switch from the traditional Marxist-Leninist ideology only very recently. Indeed, Marchais admitted that the PCF had changed and is likely to change even more in the future.[6]

In Spain the Communist Party was legalized only in the spring of 1977. But its chief, Santiago Carillo, has quickly become a staunch supporter of Eurocommunism and expressed himself strongly in favor of a "democratic, parliamentary multi-party socialism."[7]

Various statements of the leadership of the Communist parties in Italy, France, and Spain stress their commitment to the new ideas. The economic specialist of the CPI, Giorgio Napolitano, declared that in Italy no further nationalizations of industry were envisaged, and that the state in its planning would have to create the conditions to induce private investments in sectors considered essential for Italy's economic welfare. Special incentives for such investments would be offered, including favorable credits.[8] All three parties have sharply criticized the despotic conditions in the Soviet Union and deplored the violation of human rights of dissidents in that and other East European countries. They have condemned the 1968 invasion of Czechoslovakia by Soviet armed forces and proclaimed the principle of their independence from the Soviet Union, but they have not made a clear break with the sister party in the USSR. No real schism exists between Moscow and the Eurocommunists and, of course, there is no empirical evidence whether Eurocommunism can become a viable ideology of its own or will remain nothing more than a variation of European socialism. In the meantime, Eurocommunism may have deleterious effects upon the loyalty of the satellite regimes of Eastern Europe to the Soviet Union. Their leaders are likely to sympathize in the bottom of their hearts with the tendencies toward autonomy shown by the communist parties of Italy, Spain, and France and wish for a similar status for themselves with an accompanying relaxation of Soviet domination.

While it is always possible that Eurocommunism represents a departure from Soviet totalitarianism, at present this is an untested assumption. The important question is not how the Eurocommunists behave when they are outside the government working to participate in its control, but what actions they will take when they are in power or favorably positioned to exercise power. When the latter happens, the old undemocratic, staunchly pro-Soviet face may reemerge. This is a true dilemma for the present leaders and people, especially of Italy and France, which will be discussed further in our essays on the Italian and French socialist parties.

NATIONAL PATTERNS OF SOCIALIST PARTY INVOLVEMENT

Before concluding our introductory comments, it might be useful to describe briefly four categories of involvement by West European socialist parties in their national political systems. This involvement depends to a large extent on their own popular support as well as the strength and number of competing parties.[9]

1. The socialist party is the dominant party that has controlled the government for several decades, is supported by approximately 40 percent of the electorate, and frequently had an absolute majority in the legislature. Sweden has been the typical example, but a nonsocialist government is in power since 1976. However, recent public opinion polls suggest a swing back to a socialist party majority.[10] Norway also fits into this category; the traditional Labour Party (DNA), except for a couple of breaks in the 1960s and the beginning of the 1970s, formed the government for all the time, having had an absolute majority in the Storting until 1971. After the general elections of 1973, the DNA reduced its strength in the Storting from 74 to 62 (out of 155), and formed a minority government that still remains in power. Polls taken at the beginning of 1977 indicate a strong upward trend for the DNA.[11]

2. The socialist party is one of the main parties in an essentially two-party system. Britain is obviously the long-standing prototype, and so is Austria. West Germany also falls into this category with the Liberals (FDP) having been *so far* the faithful ally of the SPD. Change in governmental control requires only a relatively small shift in the votes of the electorate.

3. The socialist party is a member of a coalition comprising one or several nonsocialist parties. Belgium, The Netherlands, and Denmark have been typical examples of this category. Until 1976 such a situation also prevailed in Italy.

4. The socialist party, together with the communist party, for a number of years, has remained in the opposition vis-a-vis a coalition of nonsocialist middle-of-the-road rightist parties. Frence is the typical case, although this may change after the March 1978 elections.

The situation in Portugal is too new to categorize the Soares minority government of the Socialist Party. In Spain, the Socialist Workers Party, under Felipe Gonzales the second strongest party receiving nearly 29 percent of the vote in the June 1977 elections, is the major opposition party vis-a-vis the government of Prime Minister Adolfo Suarez and his Union of the Democratic Center, which polled 31 percent.[12] Since Suarez' party does not have a majority in the Chamber of Deputies, a later coalition government with the Socialists can not be entirely discarded.

NOTES

1. *International Herald-Tribune*, May 5, 1977.
2. They received 53% of the vote in the municipal elections and took more than two-thirds of the municipal positions in France. (*International Herald-Tribune*, May 4, 1977).
3. *International Herald-Tribune*, May 10, 1977.
4. James May, "Is There a European Socialism?" *Journal of Common Market Studies*, vol. XIII, no. 4 (June 1975): 492–502. See also Norber Gresch, "Die Zusammenarbeit der Parteien des demokratischen Sozialismus in Westeuropa," in *Europaische Schriften*, vol. 42/43 (Bonn: Institut für Europaische Politik, 1976), pp. 149–249.
5. May, op. cit., pp. 501–02.
6. *Der Spiegel*, vol. 31, no. 20 (May 9, 1977), p. 172.
7. Ibid., p. 171.
8. Ibid., p. 178.
9. This typology is taken from Guy de Carmoy's paper presented at the CAS Stirling University Conference, August 12–14, 1976, and entitled "Concepts, Instruments, and Strategies of Socialism in Western Europe.
10. Public opinion polls in Sweden taken in early 1977 indicate a swing back to the socialists after they had lost control of the government in the 1976 elections. They increased their strength from 42.7 percent to 49 percent, while nonsocialist parties declined from 50.8 to 46.5 percent (*International Herald-Tribune*, May 4, 1977).
11. See the chapter by Martin Saeter included in this volume.
12. *International Herald-Tribune*, June 18–19, 1977, p. 1.

CHAPTER

2

THE LABOUR PARTY AND BRITISH FOREIGN POLICY

John Roper

Twenty-five years ago the outgoing International Secretary of the Labour Party was able to write in a collection of *New Fabian Essays*

> The very success of Fabianism as an instrument of domestic reform condemns it as a guide to world politics. The world as a whole has never resembled the delicately integrated democracy which Britain developed in the three centuries following the Civil War—nor have more than a tiny minority of the states within it. *Leviathan* is still a better handbook for foreign affairs than *Fabian Essays*. An understanding of the power element in politics is the first necessity for a sound foreign policy.

So wrote Denis Healey in 1951 and he went on to say that the other main contributor to British Socialism, the trade union movement, could still go some way "to filling the gap in Fabian theory" even if it was more afflicted by parochialism than the Fabians and tended "to intervene in the formation of foreign policy to correct errors rather than to give positive direction."

Then as now the major influences on Labour Party thinking about world affairs have come from neither the Fabians nor the trade unions, but from the Liberal-Nonconformist wing with its bias towards pacifism, and the neo-Marxist wing. For the benefit of those not altogether acquainted with the ornithology of the Labour Party, I should perhaps add that it has always been permitted to have a multiplicity of wings.

The substantive point that Healey was making was that as the party lacked any systematic theory of world affairs, it has "too often fallen victim to the besetting sin of all progressive movements—utopianism."

A great deal of this description would still appear relevant; in particular in opposition a great deal of the party ignores foreign affairs and the "utopian" minority encourages the adoption of policies that can create problems for Labour governments when they come to office.

On the other hand, when the party has come into office in 1964 and 1974, the Prime Minister has ensured that the Foreign and Defense portfolios have been given not necessarily to those who have said the most in opposition but to ministers on the center or right of the party who are likely to temper the party's natural utopianism with a fairly hard dose of realism. This has of course led to disagreement from time to time between the government and the party's Annual Conference.

The National Executive Committee, which is made up largely of representatives elected in two sections by the trade unions and constituency parties, has been for the last 10 years a body with a political center of gravity to the left of that of the Parliamentary Labour Party. Only a small minority of its members are members of Parliament and even of those who are, less than half are ministers, almost all those who are not being members of the left-wing Tribune Group.

The Party Conference, which meets once a year in the autumn, is dominated in terms of votes by the trade unions and in general is more open to influence, direct or indirect, by the government when a Labour government is in office. This has not prevented the Conference from taking up positions on foreign policy different from those of the government from time to time as in the 1964–1970 Labour Government over criticisms of United States policy in Vietnam and in 1975 at the Special Conference prior to the referendum on continued membership of the European Community where the party committed itself to campaign against continued membership, while the Government was recommending a "yes" vote.

The position of the National Executive Committee and the differences in its position from those of the Government can be seen very clearly in the policy document "Labour's Programme 1976" debated at the 1976 party conference. As has been widely reported, the Prime Minister had very considerable objections to substantial parts of this document both in its domestic and foreign policy sections, and the Party's General Secretary, Ron Hayward, has had to include in his foreword a qualifying paragraph saying,

> We are aware that there are policies and priorities outlined in this document on which the Government takes a different view. These differences have been the subject of considerable discussion between the National Executive Committee and the Government, and these discussions will continue in the future.

In the fields of foreign and defense policy three examples of significant differences between the Government and Party are the attitudes to direct elections to the European Parliament, the level of defense expenditures and attitude towards Namibia or Southwest Africa. The first two of these are elements of the Party's attitude towards European integration and Atlantic defense cooperation that will be examined in more detail later. On direct elections, the Government while making clear its resistance to any change in the powers of the European Parliament believes it has a treaty obligation to agree to direct elections; the party's National Executive Committee, on the other hand, has made a recommendation to the party conference by 17 votes to 3 that the party should oppose direct elections in principle on the ground that it is a step towards federalism.

While the Labour Government has revised downwards the defense spending plans that they inherited from their predecessors, this has not resulted in any significant fall in the level of defense spending in recent times, but rather a cutback in the rate of increase that was planned, a deferment in procurement of some weapons systems, and an acceleration of withdrawals from the Indian Ocean and Mediterranean. These cuts although heavily criticized by the opposition are considered to be far from adequate by the National Executive who want to see reductions of 1000 million pounds, or some 20 percent of present spending. The policy document (pp. 114–115) reports on detailed proposals that it has adopted on the recommendation of a study group in which Ministry of Defense ministers refused to take part. The 1000-million-pound cut could be achieved by "the removal from the present defense program of the provision for Polaris (the Nuclear Missile Submarine), and facilities and Army Combat Forces outside Europe—which presumably means the three battalions in Hong Kong. In addition, there would have to be major cuts from two of the three services. In the case of the army this would involve reducing BAORs (British Army of the Rhine's) strength from 55,000 to 30,000, in breach of the Brussels Treaty, for the RAF the scrapping of the MRCA (Multirole Combat Aircraft) program and for the navy the paying off of large surface ships and changes in the new ship construction program including the second and third ASW (antisubmarine warfare) cruisers. These proposals are of course vehemently opposed by Labour defense ministers and by the Prime Minister, but the fact that they are being put forward by the party which is in Government could cause a good deal of confusion among those abroad.

Finally, in the case of South Africa and South West Africa (Namibia) there is agreement between Government and Party about our repugnance to apartheid, but considerable differences about the measures to be adopted. For example, the National Executive Committee wishes the

Government to amend or terminate the agreement that exists between the nationalized Atomic Energy Authority and Rio Tinto Zinc over the uranium mines at Rossing in Namibia so that we do not receive the uranium supplies from Namibia while it is still under illegal South African control. This the Government has consistently refused to do.

These three examples of the differences in policy between the Labour Government and the Labour Party as represented by the National Executive Committee give some indication of the difficult task of party management that falls to a Labour Prime Minister. In some respects, they are now sharper than they have been in recent years, reflecting in part a steady move to the left in recent years of the National Executive Committee, but this has clearly been made more apparent by the preparation of the policy compendium. It has been suggested that James Callaghan will adopt a different aproach to party management to that of his predecessor, but no politician will court confrontation with his party. He is therefore caught in something of a dilemma if, as I believe, he feels that the policies in "Labour's Programme 1976" in the domestic as well as the foreign affairs field will be electorally damaging.

It would be wrong, on the other hand, to place too much emphasis in terms of current political power on this role of the National Executive Committee. Within the 300 members of the Parliamentary Labour Party there is a substantial majority in favor of the policies of the Government on defense matters and on most foreign policy matters (direct elections). There is a vocal minority—broadly the members of the Left-Wing Tribune Group—but their weakness within the Parliamentary Labour Party is shown by the fact that they are unable to elect a single member of the so-called Liaison Committee that represents back-bench Labour members in their dealings with the Government.

There is one other area in which the political attitudes of the National Executive Committee can have some importance, and that does have relation to the transnational links of socialist parties. The Labour Party initially took the view that they should not participate as members or observers of the Confederation of Socialist Parties of the European Community following British accession on the grounds that British membership had not yet been confirmed by the free vote of the British people (this paralleled the decision of Labour M.P.s not to take up their seats in the European Parliament). In fact, the decision to take part in the Confederation was postponed by the NEC until March of 1976, although Jenny Little, International Secretary of the Party, had attended as an observer the meeting in Denmark on 18 January 1976. When the party did attend its first meeting on March 31, 1976, in Brussels, it considerably disappointed the other parties by refusing to nominate members to serve on the working party to prepare the electoral platform for the Socialist candidates for direct election to the European Parliament or to the four subgroups working on specific topics. This was on the grounds that the party had not yet considered what its attitude was to direct elections. The party's representatives on the Bureau of the Confederation are Ian Mikardo and Alec Kitson, both staunch anti-Europeans. As the party conference has decided against the principle of direct elections, their position in the Confederation will be a difficult one, whatever effect such a decision may have in Westminster.

I should like in the rest of what I have to say to look at the party's positions in relation to the Atlantic Security System and European integration. We find that on the first of these, in terms of its behavior in government and its leaders' statements in opposition, it has been as strong a supporter as any social democratic party, whereas when it comes to European integration it has taken an equivocal, or some would say negative, approach, being at best a reluctant European.

The reason for both of these attitudes can, I think, be found in the development of foreign policy attitudes in the immediate postwar period. It would be wrong to give Ernest Bevin all the credit for the creation of the Atlantic Alliance, but probably his greatest contribution to British foreign policy was in helping to build that alliance. Although that policy was not universally popular in the Labour Party at the time, and indeed rearmament in 1951 led to Nye Bevan and Harold Wilson leaving the Government, the commitment to a collective defense has been a firm one in the party ever since. That is not, of course, to deny that vocal utopian minorities have not maintained their presence in the parties or that it is usually easier to get a cheer at party conferences for a speech that talks about cuts in the defense budget than one that talks about cuts in the education or social service budget. Party Conference has from time to time passed resolutions calling for the withdrawal of U.S. nuclear bases from Britain, but these have been studiously ignored by Labour governments. Party Conference has always rejected firmly any resolution calling for withdrawal from NATO, although it has accepted general statements of principle about the ultimate objective being the mutual and concurrent phasing out of NATO and the Warsaw Pact. Defense is nowhere popular but it is accepted as a necessary evil by a clear majority of the party.

Labour governments have always behaved as the heirs of Ernest Bevin, Harold Wilson in 1974/75 repeatedly claiming that Anglo-American relations were so much better under a Labour government than they had been under the Conservatives. Callaghan, at the same time, in private if not in public, gave the impression that one of the reasons he was skeptical about the Common Market was that he was not certain it was compatible with strong transatlantic ties. Similarly, Labour Defence ministers, Denis Healey in the 1964–70 Labour Government and Roy Mason in 1974–76, have been among those most active in supporting standardization and closer cooperation within the alliance. The Eurogroup arose from an initiative of Denis Healey and both he and Roy Mason, in successive defense reviews, have done their best to ensure that the British contribution to NATO is maintained. Roy Mason, as chairman of Eurogroup last year, attempted to popularize the concept of the "two-way street" as a mechanism to rationalize defense procurement across the Atlantic. He also played an active part in evolving a European defense procurement forum in which France can take part. On a bilateral basis his success in agreeing on a memorandum of understanding with the United States that will enable UK suppliers to override the "Buy America Act" when tendering for U.S. defense contracts is an important practical step towards commonality in procurement, and could provide a model for a more general system of common procurement for the alliance.

The Labour Party has therefore accepted the need for common defense and Labour governments have worked to make it effective. Why then has Labour adopted a so-much-more-skeptical attitude to European integration? If one goes back to the immediate postwar period, one sees a long history of distrust. Although there was a minority of "Europeans," the European Movement was looked at with some suspicion from the start—the Hague Congress in 1948—as some gimmick of Churchill's and the Tories. Healey, writing in 1951, provided an explanation for the party's attitude at that time that also explains much of the subsequent reluctance. After considering the difficulty of cooperation between trade unions at an international level, he wrote

> Democratic Socialism is even less widespread and powerful than trade unionism and even more colored by national interests. Every Democratic Socialist party aims primarily at power in its own nation state and is thus obliged to consider the interests of its own state first. Indeed to the extent that the internal structure of a state satisfies the interests of the workers within it, to that extent its socialist party will tend to put the national interest before international solidarity. It is no accident that in their approach to European Unity since 1945 the socialist parties of Britain and Scandinavia have been the most conservative—for they have the most to conserve. Economic factors reinforce the trend towards nationalism in a governing socialist party: in a world predominantly capitalist, national economic planning may often be inconsistent with forms of international cooperation a *laissez-faire* government would be quite willing to accept.

It was a combination of three factors—a belief in British Social-Democratic superiority, a feeling that it was easier to build socialism or social democracy in one country than in a "capitalist club," and misgivings that membership of the Economic Community would lock us into a rigid block committed to the maintenance of the cold war in Europe—that fueled the anti-European forces in the Labour Party. It was not strictly speaking a Left-Right decision in traditional Labour Party terms, although with rare exceptions (mainly old-guard internationalists with an ILP background) the left took an anti-Market position. The center and right of the party were split and their division on this issue strengthened the position of the left in the party in the period 1970–75. This division had become apparent as early as 1962 at the time of the first British application by the Macmillan Government when Hugh Gaitskell had made a fighting speech against British membership at the Labour Party Conference. The Labour Government of 1964–70 was persuaded whilst in office of the logic of the case for British membership and made the second application, but were then able in 1971, in opposition, to swing against "the Tory terms." How far this position of Harold Wilson was an exercise in party management it is not easy to say, but it certainly helped him, together with the reaction to the Conservative Government's Industrial Relations Act, to rebuild his links with the trade unions that had been badly strained during the closing years of his own administration. Reelection in 1975 with the commitment to renegotiation and a referendum presented him with a final opportunity to demonstrate his Houdini-like powers before this year's retirement. The political gymnastics that made this possible without a total loss of credibility was far from easy for the party to follow. As has been seen, there is still a strong antiintegration majority among the NEC and probably to a lesser extent in the party conference in spite of the active involvement of many of the trade unions in European institutions. In the Parliamentary Labour Party there is still a core of 25 percent opposed to the Community and any further integration, including several of the present Labour members of the European Parliament. On the other side there are some 10–15 percent who, if not committed federalists, are anxious to see early steps to further integration. In between there are the bulk of the party who follow broadly the position of the Prime Minister, which might be described as one of pragmatic minimalism. He is prepared to see further steps towards integration, but each one of them has to be justified in its own right as providing clear benefits for the United Kingdom. He has shown himself resistant to any institutional developments such as moving to majority voting, and when asked about the commitment to "economic and monetary union" he suggested it had as much reality or likelihood of being achieved as the objective of general and complete disarmament that we annually espouse in United Nations General Assembly resolutions.

On the other hand, it may be that membership of the Community will have an educational effect upon ministers. Certainly some of the junior ministers who were actively opposed to membership prior to 1974 have begun to see departmental advantages in continued British membership. In the party in the country, one finds a grudging acceptance of the referendum combined with a wish that the matter would now go away. Certainly such an attitude might affect party activity in an election campaign for the European Parliament. How far it extends to Labour voters as well as to Labour activists it is difficult to assess but the opponents of direct elections on the National Executive have certainly adduced the argument of low Labour turnout leading to massive Tory victories as one of the covert arguments against such elections.

In conclusion, therefore, one seems within the Labour Party to have foreign policy attitudes not necessarily very different from those in the Danish and Norwegian Labour parties, but apparently sharply different from those of Continental Europe, whether North or South. Does this suggest that our parties should be divided into three categories and not the two divisions of North and South that are usually adopted?

CHAPTER

3

THE SOCIAL DEMOCRATIC PARTY AND WEST GERMAN FOREIGN POLICY: CONTINUITY AND CHANGE

Charles R. Foster

Since the early days of the Federal Republic, foreign policy of the Social Democratic Party has undergone profound change. In the early 1950s, reunification was the paramount policy issue for the SPD. Pursuit of the phantom of reunification led the party to rejection of close ties with both the United States and Western Europe and eventually to domestic party paralysis. By the late 1960s the party had undergone a major internal rapprochement with the East based on acceptance of the postwar status quo, a close alliance with the United States, and integration with its Western neighbors.[1]

The changes in SPD policy and the party's two-step accession to power in the 1960s were the result of a complex linkage of a changing international environment and domestic political forces. That is to say, the change in the Social Democratic Party power structure, without which the *Ostpolitik* would not have been possible, was a function of both a changed international environment and domestic political evolution. The SPD played a pivotal role in the coming of age of the Federal Republic as the special nature of FRG (Federal Republic of Germany) foreign relations was gradually superseded by a more normal set of relationships. This can be most easily observed in the changed relations with the Soviet Union and its Eastern European allies, but it is also clearly present in Atlantic and West European relations.

A review of the party's program shows remarkably little attention to foreign and military affairs. Historically, foreign policy had been largely

---

I am very much indebted to the research assistance of Douglas Bergner, M.A. (Johns Hopkins University). Parts of this chapter are based on an unpublished paper by Bergner.

outside the mainstream of its ideological development. At the Wennigsen Conference in 1945, Schumacher established the principles that were to dominate the party's postwar foreign policy. He and, after his death in 1952, Erlich Ollenhauer resolutely maintained that the reunification issue was the most critical determinant of policy. Foremost was the demand for "the full maintenance of the internal and external sovereignty of the German people."[2] Germany was to be treated as an equal. In practice this was to mean the rejection of all European institutions based on other than Schumacher's terms: full equality; cooperation with all European nations committed to social democratic principles; and, most importantly, rejection of the CDU's claim that reunification could be achieved through integration with the West. Thus, the Schuman Plan (1950), the EDC (European Defense Community; 1952–54), and the WEU (Western European Union)-NATO solution to the rearmament question (1954–55) were all fiercely opposed by the SPD. Integration into the West was further complicated for the SPD by the fact that much of its prewar base of political support was lost to the East through the partition and the fact that the Catholic Europe of the Six seemed too restricted and conservative. It was the rearmament issue, which spanned more than four years, that provided both the key to Adenauer's politics of integration into the West and restoration of full sovereignty as well as the focal point of SPD opposition. Adenauer's West-oriented policies (both toward the United States and Western Europe) forced the SPD into a position of opposition on virtually all fronts, an opposition that over time grew to be sterile and dogmatic. The strength of the reunification issue gradually receded as the refugees were integrated into the society and the economy boomed.

The SPD was fundamentally neither anti-Western, pacifist, nor Communist-oriented. It would have preferred, however, to give more attention to overtures from the East concerning restoration of a united and neutral Germany (for example, the Soviet note of March, 1952). Its goal was a neutral, socialist, democratic Germany that, by virtue of its geographic, economic, and social position between East and West, would have acted to reduce the ever-increasing polarization in Europe and the world. This goal, however, overlooked the crucial importance of control over Germany, the loss of which neither West nor East could afford. The size and economic strength of Germany, to say nothing of the fear of a revival of an independent Germany, forced both the West and the Soviet Union to reject the concept of a neutral, reunited Germany. An "Austrian solution," while attractive to some Germans, found no favor elsewhere.

The very success of Adenauer's policies made the SPD opposition seem ever more unrealistic and doctrinaire. The economic recovery took hold and, over time, destroyed much of the popular support for a socialized economy that had existed throughout wide ranges of the society.[3] The attainment of full sovereignty as a result of the 1954 Paris treaties, even if at the cost of rearmament, further strengthened Adenauer's claim to successful leadership. The fact that Adenauer's policies meshed nicely with U.S. goals in Europe—strengthening the defense and socioeconomic bases of European society—also was politically valuable for the CDU, as the United States occasionally took a less than nonpartisan position in German domestic political affairs.[4]

The deteriorating political position of the SPD relative to the CDU/CSU can best be seen in the actual election returns listed in Table 3.1. After barely losing the first Bundestag election, the relative position of the SPD declined precipitously. After the 1957 election, in which the CDU/CSU won an absolute majority, the SPD began a period of significant internal transformation.

TABLE 3.1

Bundestag Election Results
(in percent)

	1949	1953	1957
CDU/CSU	31.0	45.2	50.2
SPD	29.2	28.8	31.8
FPD	11.9	9.5	7.7
Other	27.9	16.5	10.3

Source: Adapted from O.K. Flechtheim, *Die Parteien der Bundesrepublik Deutschland* (Hamburg: Hoffman and Canpe, 1973), p. 59.

The strength of the older party functionaries under Ollenhauer was challenged by a group of generally younger and more moderate, pragmatic politicians. The first major shift in SPD policy occurred in 1957. After considerable intraparty discussions, the party voted to support the Treaty of Rome for the creation of the European Economic Community. This marked the acceptance of integration into the West without a prior settlement of the reunification question. The move was justified on a wide variety of economic grounds and, though perhaps somewhat contradictorily, was not seen as obstructing an eventual Eastern settlement.

Nineteen fifty-nine was the watershed year with the announcement of the *Deutschlandplan* and the Godesberg Program. The *Deutschlandplan* was, in effect, the last gasp of the old policy. In it, the SPD proposed a three-step unification plan starting with the withdrawal of all foreign troops, establishment of a German confederation based on the two states as equals, and free elections and political activity. The lack of response from the East to this offer, the most generous possible from the SPD, made it clear that the Social Democratic approach to reunification was not consonant with Soviet interests, and hence had no future.[5]

The moderate Godesberg Program, though not primarily a foreign policy document, was significant in terms of its reversal of much of the previously hallowed ideological doctrine of the SPD. It signaled the victory of the moderate, pragmatic wing of the party led by Wehner, Erler, and Brandt. In foreign policy, it proposed a zone of "relaxation" for Europe and suggested establishment of diplomatic relations with all nations regardless of their type of social system.[6] At Godesberg, also, the party acknowledged its de facto commitment to national defense, and it rejected a showing demanded from its pacifist wing for the withdrawal of atomic weapons from West Germany on the ground that this might lead to an American retreat from Europe.

The transition of the SPD continued in 1960 as Herbert Wehner broke radically with the past in a speech to the ***Bundestag*** on June 30. Speaking for the party, Wehner announced the full acceptance by the SPD of both the European and Atlantic policies of the CDU/CSU.[7] This brought the party in line with the current commitments of the FRG and made possible a functioning system of alternating two-party rule.

By the time of the 1961 election, the SPD had effectively completed its reorientation. NATO, the EEC, and Germany's Western integration were all part of the SPD platform. And the Chancellor candidate was West Berlin Mayor Willy Brandt (though Brandt did not become party chairman until Ollenhauer's death in 1964). The 1961 Berlin Crisis, which reemphasized Germany's dependence on the West and the untenability of a neutralist position, removed the last lingering doubts about integrating the FRG into the West.

POLICY TRENDS TOWARD THE WEST

From the time of the full acceptance of the Federal Republic's European policies, the SPD position evolved to active promotion of Western integration. At both the Hague and Paris Summits (December 1969, and October 1972), the SPD supported the ambitious goals of the EC, including full economic and monetary union of the Nine by 1980.

The Hannover Party Congress of April 1973 adopted a draft of a program framework that included an endorsement of the European integration process and attempted to reconcile the desire for long-term domestic sociopolitical progress with the gradually increasing economic interdependence of the nine still distinctly national policies. The framework also stated that aspects of economic policy could be best realized at the European level and that the party would be ready to transfer elements of sovereignty to democratically organized supranational institutions. Furthermore, the framework recommended closer transnational cooperation among Social Democratic parties in the EC. Despite criticism by some Young Socialists that integration had thus far only been of benefit to industry and capital, the great majority at the meeting supported a moderate reformist position.[8]

Since 1973, and, not by coincidence, since the oil crisis, SPD enthusiasm for further integration has waned slightly. The response to the oil crisis by the various EC members indicated the continuing strength of *national* economic interests and revealed the superficiality of the declarations of The Hague and Paris. Progress toward integration remains one of the keystones of SPD rhetoric, but events during and after the oil crisis have served as a sobering reminder of the long distance yet to be traveled before the EC speaks with one voice.

At a special SPD conference on foreign policy in January 1975 Chancellor Helmut Schmidt again voiced strong support for EC cooperation and stressed the Federal Republic's willingness to continue its financial commitment. But significantly, Schmidt cautioned about the prospects for implementation of a common social democratic foreign policy. And Wischnewski, a top aid to Schmidt who chaired the discussion on the EC, warned that there was need for reform, both of the administrative *apparat* in Brussels and of the common agricultural policy.

In September 1975 the SPD issued a report on European policy that called for more democratic decision making in the EC as well as for a gradual leveling of regional differences and closer contact among the social democratic and socialist parties of Europe.

Another special conference on international politics was held by the SPD in April 1976. Willy Brandt keynoted the conference with a long speech on 10 years of Social Democratic foreign policy and announced once again that he would compete for a seat in the European Parliament.

Since the formation in 1974 of a coalition of social democratic and socialist parties of Europe, the issue of SPD relations with these other parties has grown in importance, especially in light of the projected direct election of a European Parliament in 1978. The Dutch sought the immediate establishment of a European socialist party while the SPD favored a more cautious approach, looking toward a gradual harmonization of programs but maintaining the full autonomy of each party. A crucial difference, of course, was the SPD refusal to take any common action, much less form a popular front with communists. There are other policy differences, such as codetermination, that create major stumbling blocks to the creation of a common socialist platform in a European Parliament.[9] It is likely that direct elections to this Parliament will tend to fragment the superficial unity of the socialist party group. The question of the SPD relations with other socialist parties of Europe is perhaps the most crucial facing the party in the next decade, made especially acute by the possible rise to power of popular-front governments in France and Italy.

POLICY TOWARD THE EAST

In the early 1960s the SPD, still in opposition, found itself more closely aligned with the FDP and the left wing of the CDU on foreign policy questions. Throughout the early and mid-1960s there was continuous discussion within the SPD on the nature of detente policies and on the extent to which the FRG should pursue new initiatives. By June 1966, at its annual party conference, the SPD was able to announce a program incorporating major revisions of policy. After analyzing the failure of previous policies to achieve reunification and stressing the changing international context, the party proposed pursuing close relations at all levels with the GDR (German Democratic Republic) as the best way to keep the reunification option open for some future date. They further proposed revision of the Hallstein Doctrine,[10] invalidation of the Munich Agreement, acceptance of the Oder-Neisse line, and unequivocal reunification of nuclear weapons. Thus, as early as 1966, the SPD principles for the later development of detente policy and the German *Ostpolitik* were clear.[11]

Full implementation of the SPD proposals, however, had to wait until after the 1969 elections and the accession to power of the SPD-FDP coalition. The period between 1966 and 1969, during which the SPD and the CDU/CSU governed as the "Grand Coalition," was a time of only limited foreign policy development. The constraints of coalition politics restricted the SPD in its attempts to realize the goals incorporated into the 1966 Party platform. A modification of the Hallstein Doctrine was achieved leading to the exchange of ambassadors with Rumania. However, the unwillingness to come to terms with the GDR generally held the *Ostpolitik* of the Grand Coalition in check.

The *Ostpolitik* of Brandt was based on a new premise. In contrast to the Erhard-Schroeder policies that sought to put pressure on the East German regime by coming to terms with the other East-bloc states, the policies of Brandt and the SPD recognized the necessity of reaching some sort of understanding with the GDR. It is beyond the scope of this paper to present a detailed narrative of the implementation of the SPD *Ostpolitik*.[12] It is sufficient to note that between 1969 and 1973 the SPD leadership was able to conclude the Eastern treaties with the Soviet Union, Poland, and Czechoslovakia; the Four Power Agreement on

Berlin; and the inner German Basic Treaty based on the 1966 Party platform resulting in a de facto (though not de jure) recognition of the GDR.

The SPD *Ostpolitik* can be viewed simply as a realignment of German foreign policy with the U.S. determination to reduce tension in Europe by acceptance of the status quo. But the *Ostpolitik* can perhaps be better seen as a means and not an end in itself.

For Brandt, the *Ostpolitik* was to be the German contribution to a general effort aimed at establishment of a "European Peace Order." This would be achieved by a two-step process: first, a period of regulated coexistence *(geregeltes Nebeneinander)* and, eventually, attainment of organization for cooperation *(Organizierung des Miteinanders)*. The European Peace Order would be a structure superimposed on the blocs that would gradually break down differences between them and make war unthinkable. The role of national boundaries would become less significant, and the two parts of Germany would eventually enter into some sort of confederal arrangement.[13]

A conservative critic, Walter Hahn, has suggested that Egon Bahr, sometimes called the "chief architect" of Brandt's *Ostpolitik*, had even more ambitious *Ostpolitik* goals.[14] A European settlement based on mutual recognition and reduction of tensions would eventually lead to the end of superpower hegemony in Europe. The European states would be free again to determine their own destiny. Such a situation would likely be most conducive to German reunification.

Thus, although the tactics differed, both the early postwar Social Democratic foreign policy and the Brandt-Bahr *Ostpolitik* seemed aimed at achieving reunification and restoration of an active German role in Central Europe. There is more than coincidence behind Schumacher's vision of a neutral Germany and Bahr's vision of a neutral Europe.

Today, however, an active continuation of the *Ostpolitik* seems a more remote goal of the SPD leadership. The current lack of movement in the *Ostpolitik*, while in part a function of the international environment, is also due to the stronger West German nationalism and Western orientation of Helmut Schmidt and his "Hamburg Mafia."

The most important development of the *Ostpolitik* under Schmidt has been the Polish-West German Treaty of 1976. Other progress has been disappointing and rather mundane in comparison to the Brandt years. Bilaterally, the various cultural, scientific, and technological exchanges are continuing; and trade (though now slowing) has been greatly expanded. To a great extent, future German initiatives are dependent on the success of today's multilateral encounters, such as MBFR (Mutual and Balanced Reduction of Forces), the European Security Conference, and SALT, in affecting the overall environment.

The *Ostpolitik* was made possible by the development of a West German national consciousness and a remade political culture that facilitated the rise to power of the SPD.[15] The foreign policy consensus of the SPD played an important integrative function in the party, especially in the period 1959 to 1969. All ideological shadings within the party could agree on the need for detente vis-a-vis the East and the consequent integration into the larger framework of Western diplomacy.

Foreign policy, however, has lost much importance both with the general public and the party. There are now relatively few foreign policy experts in the SPD leadership. The new dominance of economic and monetary issues in foreign policy are less glamorous and evoke less discussion within the party. It may well be that tensions within the party will increase as the "policy of little steps" toward the East slows down further.

The unity of the SPD is currently maintained on policy issues in governing, but is nevertheless not something that can be taken for granted. There exists a very real tension between the more moderate sections of the party—those now dominant in Bonn—and various groupings further to the Left, that is, between the SPD in Bonn and the party in its entirety. The Young Socialists, largest opposition group within the SPD, have made clear their discontent with the direction and content of some current SPD policies. They not only would prefer to see a less capitalist-oriented EC but also favor a reassessment of the FRG's membership in NATO, including its implications for the possibility of achieving a socialist democracy. In addition, there are occasional differences in orientation between those in Bonn and some SPD leaders at the state and local levels.

The small margin of seats in the Bundestag that allows the SPD (with the FDP) to continue in power encourages party discipline in the Parliament. SPD party congresses have traditionally been the scenes of internal discussions, and it seems safe to assume this will continue.[16] The problem of SPD relations with other socialist and even communist groups of the EC will likely be one of the major issues discussed within the party in the future. If the European socialist parties make further gains, as is likely in France and Holland, the SPD will be faced with more internal and external demands for common stands on European and international issues. Even today the Dutch, French, and Italian socialist members of the European Parliament are urging the SPD to join with them in alliance with the communist members in Strasbourg. This has been resisted by the SPD, although some party politicians, such as Jochen Steffen (a Marxist) favor it. An additional issue of intraparty debate may be relations with United States, particularly in the economic sphere.

The real root of intraparty tension is the party leadership's role as the governing elite, which always makes their governmental role more important than their party role. In the Weimar Republic the SPD's "statesmanship" led to an abandonment of an activist policy and to various surrenders to the forces of reaction from 1914 to 1932.

For their first 100 years continental socialist parties failed to become a directing force in the major nations of Europe. They were neither able to carry through vital economic and political reform nor bar the way to fascism. One hopes that the German SPD will now willingly face its international responsibilities, eschew its historical passivity, and provide leadership in European political actions designed to maximize human welfare and overcome the European divisions.

NOTES

1. For a good general discussion of German foreign policy, see Joseph Joffe, "Foreign Policy of the German Federal Republic," in *Foreign Policy-World Politics*, ed. R. Macridis (Englewood Cliffs, N.J.: Prentice Hall, 5th ed., 1976). For a good discussion on the foreign policy resolutions of various SPD party Congresses, see Rudolf Hrbek, "The SPD vis-a-vis European Integration and Atlantic Relations," in the *Stirling Conference Proceedings* (Committee on Atlantic Studies, Washington, 1976). For a general discussion of the role of socialist parties of the European Community see the papers presented at a conference at Birmingham University on December 16–17, 1974, subsequently published in the *Journal of Common Market Studies*, vol. XIII, no. 4 (June 1975), pp. 415–501.

2. Harold K. Schellenberger, *The SPD in the Bonn Republic: A Socialist Party Modernizes* (The Hague: Martinus Nijhoff, 1968), p. 51. The earliest full statement of party policy written by Schumacher was the *Action Program of 1952*.

3. Even in the CDU. See, for example, the 1947 Program of the CDU in Ossip K. Flechtheim, *Die Parteien der Bundesrepublik Deutschland* (Hamburg: Hoffman and Canpe, 1973), pp. 157–162.

4. For U.S. interference in the 1953 election, see Roger Morgan, *The U.S. and West Germany 1945–1973* (London: Oxford University Press, 1974), pp. 41–42.

5. Wolfram Hanrieder, *The Stable Crisis* (Santa Barbara: University of Southern California Press, 1970), p. 151.

6. David Childs, *From Schumacher to Brandt* (Oxford: Pergamon Press, 1966), pp. 133–134. The "pragmatic" Godesberg program was made possible by the rise of white-collar leadership in the party, although the voting base is still heavily proletarian. See Flechtheim, op. cit., pp. 63, 401, and 405, from whom the following table is adapted:

Job Composition of Party Members and Voters (%)

	Party Members			Party Voters		
	1970 SPD	1970 CEU/CSU	1967 FDP	1969 SPD	1969 CDU/CSU	1969 FDP
Self-employed	6	31	28	5	20	27
Beamte	10	18	8	8	9	5
Angestellte	23	27	40	22	16	27
Manual Workers	37	13	14	47	35	18

7. Peter Merkl, ***German Foreign Policies, West and East*** (Santa Barbara, Calif.: Clio Press, 1974), p. 114.

8. The influence of the Juso's is smaller than reports published in the German press. They lack any substantial base among laborers, their membership being recruited almost entirely in schools and colleges. The Juso leadership has always avoided a break with the party leadership. For a discussion of the SPD left see Guenter Minnerup, "West Germany since the War," ***New Left Review*** (London), October 1976.

9. Norbe Gresch, "Die Zusammenarbeit der Parteien des demokratischen Sozialismus in Westeuropa," in *Europaische Schriften*, vol. 42/43 (Bonn: Institut für Europaische Politik, 1976), pp. 149–249.

10. The Hallstein Doctrine, named after Adenauer's first foreign secretary, enunciated the unwritten rule that diplomatic relations would be severed with any country that took up full diplomatic relations with the GDR. The doctrine became a victim of the ***Ostpolitik*** in the late 1960s.

11. Karl Kaiser, ***German Foreign Policy in Transition*** (London: Oxford University Press, 1968), pp. 101–02.

12. Helga Haftendorn, in an unpublished paper, emphasizes three dimensions of *Ostpolitik*: 1) The support for multinational detente policy—in order to avoid the "German quarrels" dominating multinational negotiations such as the CSCE,—Bonn had to achieve a modus vivendi with the East; 2) Bilateral *Ostpolitik* with Moscow, Prague, and Warsaw; 3) The domestic dimensions of *Ostpolitik*. The margin of consensus between the FDP and the SPD is greatest in foreign policy.

13. Prescott Wurlitzer, "West Germany's Ostpolitik: A Present and Future Outlook," in ***Atlantic Community Quarterly*** (Winter 1976–77), pp. 82–84.

14. Walter Hahn, "West Germany's Ostpolitik: The Grand Design of Egon Bahr," in ***Orbis*** (Winter 1973), pp. 873–80.

15. For a good discussion of how a new domestic consensus, accepting the Federal Republic as a new nation state, was framed, thus not enabling the *Ostpolitik* to dismantle some myths about reunification, see Gebhard Schweigler, *National Consciousness in Divided Germany* (London: Sage Publications, 1975), p. 287.

16. For speculation on the reemergence of ideological debate and conflict within the SPD, as part of a larger process of politicization in the FRG since 1965, see David Conradt and F. F. Mueller, "West Germany's Social Democrats since 1969," paper presented at APSA annual meeting in 1976 in Chicago.

CHAPTER

4

SOCIALIST PARTIES IN SWEDEN: FOREIGN POLICY AND NEUTRALITY

Nils Andrén

THE PREDOMINANT ROLE OF THE SOCIAL DEMOCRATS

As far as Sweden is concerned, it is not difficult to subscribe to the idea that socialist parties in Western Europe are in a key position in government. For all practical purposes the Swedish Social Democrats conducted the affairs of Sweden from September 1932 to September 1976. The only qualifications that have to be added to this assertion are that the party went out of government during the summer of 1936, leaving the affairs of the country for three summer months in the hands of a Farmers' Party "Vacation Government"; further, that there was a coalition government between the Social Democrats and the Farmers 1936–39; a national coalition government—excluding the Communists only—during the War (1939–45); and, finally, a new "red-green" coalition government 1951–57. The electoral defeat in 1976 was no landslide; the Social Democrats polled 0.9 percent less than in 1973. As the Communists lost 0.5 percent, the total shift from "left-to-right" amounted to 1.4 percent. The Social Democrats remain by far the largest party in Sweden, a position that they have held since 1914!

By all measures this represents a formidable picture of monolithic stability over a very long period. A closer look indicates, however, that the Socialists and the non-Socialists have normally been very closely balanced and that the Social Democrats at several critical junctures have been able to remain the Government party not only because of their own strength and skill but also because of certain advantages derived from the

FIGURE 4.1

Party Development in Sweden since 1944

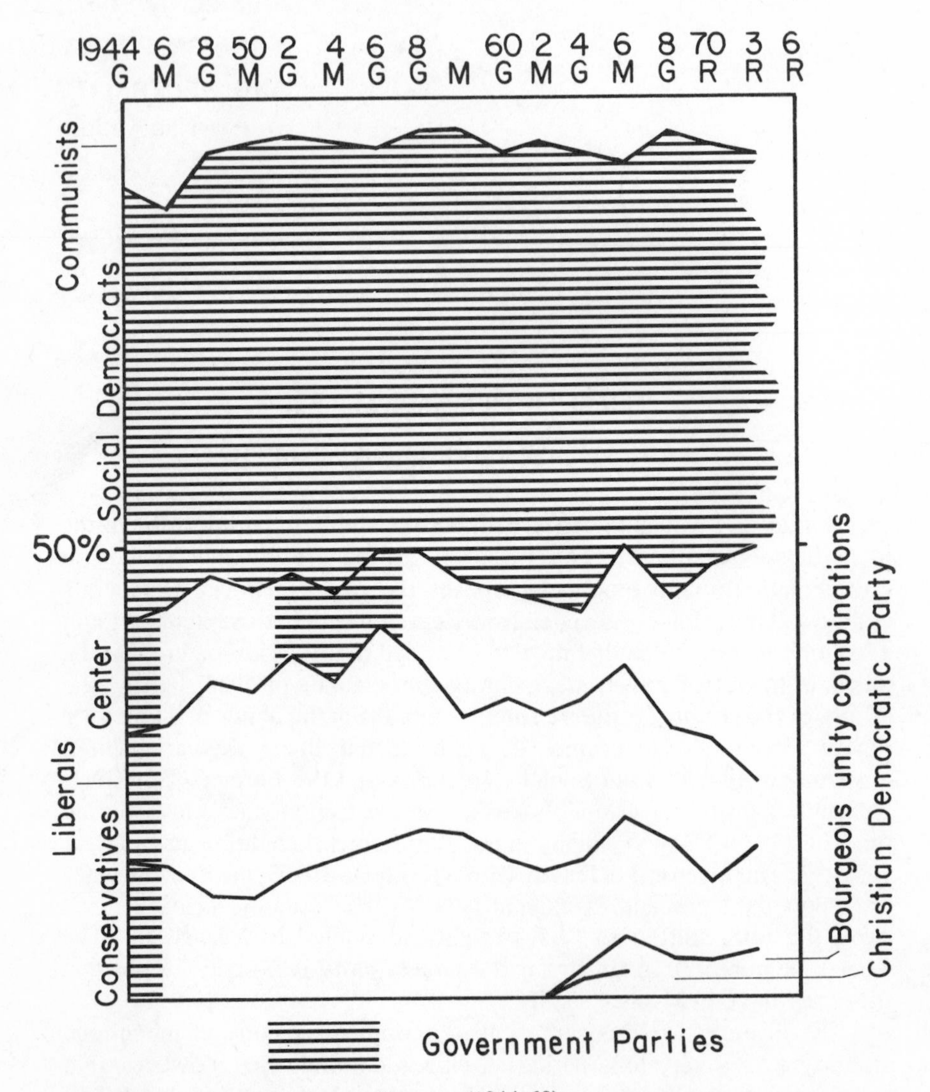

G = General elections to the Second Chamber (1944–68)

M = Elections to municipal representations, including the County Councils which served as electoral assemblies for the indirectly elected First Chamber (1946–66)

R = General elections since 1970 to the now unicameral Swedish *Riksdag*

Source: Compiled by the author.

constitutional system and the lack of skill and unwillingness to cooperate exhibited by the bourgeois parties.

Figure 4.1 illustrates the party development in Sweden since 1944. It represents the percentage of the electorate polled by the political parties 1944–76.

WHICH ARE THE SOCIALIST PARTIES?

Traditionally, two major subdivisions have been used to clarify the structure of the Swedish political party system. The first is "bourgeois"—or "nonsocialist"—parties versus socialist parties. The second subdivision, less often used since the mid-1960s, distinguishes between "democratic" parties and "nondemocratic" parties. Today the nondemocratic category includes Communists only, while all the others are democratic. In recent years the term "major parties" is often used for what was previously styled "democratic parties"—a concession to the criticism against the older terminology, primarily from its main target, the Communists. Since 1967 they have called themselves "The Left Party of the Communists" (not the Communist left party!). The moderates of the party, including the party leader at the time, would have liked to drop the "Communist" label completely. Even so, the suspicion, or even conviction, existing among the other parties and represented by the older terminology remains a political fact.*

In every analysis of the role of the Socialists in Sweden it is important to deal with the relationship between the Social Democrats and the Communists. Both parties are "labour parties" and draw the overwhelming majority of their votes from labor groups.

In actual fact, the relative significance of the labor (worker) vote is greater for the Communists than for the Social Democrats. This fact is shown in Table 4.1, on which the role of the"workers" for the nonsocialist parties as well as among the nonvoters is indicated.[1]

On the whole, the electoral profile of the Social Democrats and the

---

*This development was followed by the emergence of other communist parties to the left of the established, parliamentary Communists. The new groups, proclaiming to be the true representatives of the heritage from Marx, Lenin, and Stalin, or of the teachings of Mao, have never reached one single percent of the voters and have hence been very far from reaching the minimum 4 percent necessary for access to the *Riksdag*. In 1977 a formal split of the Left Party of the Communists took place; the "old communists" formed the Workers Communist Party, representing inter alia a less critical attitude to the Soviet Union. So far, opinion polls indicate that neither of the two Communist parties would today attract a sufficient number of votes for representation in the *Riksdag*.

TABLE 4.1

Relative Significance of the Labor (Worker) Vote, 1956-73

Party	Worker Percentage of Total Vote in					
	1956		1964		1973	
Social Democrats	64	(8)*	59	(6)*	56	(4)*
Communists	79	(7)*	78	(9)*	53	(2)*
Centre Party	13	(11)*	25	(8)*	24	(3)*
Liberal	29	(6)*	17	(5)*	18	(1)*
Conservative	7	(2)*	8	(2)*	8	(1)*
Non-Voters	51	(7)*	44	(9)*	45	(5)*

*Figures in parentheses indicate percentage of farm workers, which is included in the first figure.

Source: Allmanna valen 1973 (Swedish National Central Bureau of Statistics), pp. 90-91.

TABLE 4.2

Electoral Profile of Swedish Voters

Categories	Parties				
	SD	Com.	Cen.	Lib.	Con.
Higher administration and business	3	3	6	16	27
Farmers	1	1	21	5	11
Entrepreneurs	3	3	9	12	10
Middle rank administrators	20	18	27	38	34
Clerks, shop assistants, etc.	16	12	10	9	4
Farm workers	4	2	3	1	1
Other workers	52	51	21	17	7
Students	1	10	3	2	6

Source: Allmanna valen 1973 (Swedish National Central Bureau of Statistics), pp. 90–91.

Communists is very similar—and differs clearly from the bourgeois parties, as indicated in Table 4.2. The only major difference between the Social Democrats and the Communists is the relatively greater importance of the student vote for the Communists—which means, in fact, that in 1973 the number of students voting Communist equaled the number voting Social Democrat.

The parallelism between the two parties extends also to the geographical location of areas of major strength—always remembering that there are about ten times as many Social Democrats as Communists.

It may be emphasized that the Communists are not the major competitors of the Social Democrats for the favor of the workers' votes. For each worker voting Communist there are four voting for a nonsocialist party. However weak in parliamentary politics, the Communists have often proved formidable—but by no means invincible—adversaries in the trade union elections that for all practical purposes are dominated by the conflict between representatives of these two parties. Certainly, there are also nonsocialist members of the workers' trade unions; they play, however, a very minor role in trade union affairs.

The remarkable strength of the Communists in trade unions depends, it seems, mainly on the devotion to their work of the Communist trade union organizers and to the relative passivity of the Social Democratic rank-and-file worker. Normally, the average member sees very little difference between Social Democratic and Communist trade union leaders; in times of crisis, Communists seem, however, more ready to incite to or to take advantage of labor unrest than Social Democrats.

The historical hostility between the Communists and the Social Democrats is evidenced in Sweden as clearly as in most other countries. The origin of the present communist parties was a split first among the Social Democrats (1917) and then among the break-away group itself (1921). The numerical weakness of the Communists and their position have, in spite of all ideological disagreements, reduced them to a more or less willing supporter of the Social Democratic Governments, which they have been able to oppose consistently only when the Social Democrats by virtue of their own strength or alliances with other parties have commanded an independent majority, irrespective of Communist support.

Analyses of voters' party preferences emphasize that there is no other alternative to independent opposition except to support the Social Democrats. Seventy-five percent of all the Communists regard the Social Democrats as the "second best." Seven percent opted for the Centre

Party, but none for Liberals or Conservatives. The figures quoted illustrate the basic truth of a maxim coined by a previous Communist leader: "Our electorate would never understand a Communist policy which would lead to overthrowing a labor government." A "King's Bay" vote would be extremely unlikely in Sweden.*

THE SOCIAL DEMOCRATS BETWEEN LEFT AND CENTER: RESTRICTIONS AND POSSIBILITIES

Among the Social Democrats, 21 percent felt more affinity with the Communists than with any other party, while 44 percent gave the second position, next to their own party, to the Centre Party. The Liberals were favored by seven percent and the Conservatives by two percent.[2] These figures indicate not only that the attraction of the Communists among many Social Democrats is considerable, but also that an opening towards the "middle" is likely to be acceptable to the Social Democrats themselves. This fact indicates the possibility of an alternative mix of government parties if the present three-party coalition of nonsocialist parties would disintegrate.

Historically, the fact that the "middle area" in Swedish politics—located between Socialists and Conservatives—is divided between two parties has improved the possbilities of the Social Democrats to rally auxiliaries in times of need. This rule has applied not only when formal coalitions have been established but also, as in very recent years, in the search for more temporary parliamentary combinations in order to overcome the stalemate situation of 175 nonsocialists versus 175 Social Democrats and Communists.

It is a common mistake to think of the right-left position of the political parties as ruling their behavior on, practically speaking, all important issues. A few examples may serve to illustrate this point. Taxation has been a dominating issue in recent years—Sweden is, in fact, one of the most heavily taxed countries in the world. In recent years decisions on this matter have been carried by changing combinations between the Social Democrats and one or two of the so-called "middle parties" (the Liberal Party and the Centre Party). Some major cultural reforms have rallied the support of Social Democrats and Centrists, while on energy (especially nuclear energy) and environmental matters there is

---

*By the "King's Bay" vote, in 1963, the Gerhardsen Labour Government in Norway was defeated by a combination of bourgeois parties and Communists, and forced to resign.

fundamental agreement between the Social Democrats and their normal archenemy, the Conservatives. Add to this that the politics of compromise are not totally forgotten in Sweden; a great number of issues are decided in agreement and in others broad compromises have been possible. An important instance is the new Constitution Act, adopted in 1974.

ON SOCIOLOGICAL CONSTRAINTS

Some of the conditions creating sociological constraints have already been referred to in connection with the socialist party profile and how it differs from the nonsocialist profiles. In view of the fact that no major occupational group or interest constitutes a majority of the total population, and hence of the electorate, an important constraint consists of the fact that no party or bloc of parties can attain a parliamentary majority without considerable support from other groups. Even if the industrial workers form the largest group of supporters of the Social Democratic Party, additional support is necessary, especially from the rapidly growing group of salaried employees. These conditions may be illustrated both by the changes in the Swedish occupational structure and by the development of workers' and of other forms of trade unionism. (See Tables 4.3 and 4.4.) It is obvious that the expansion of the Central Organization of Salaried Employees and the Confederation of Professional Organizations reflects both group expansion and a growing percentage of trade union membership in the groups.

TABLE 4.3

Changes in Swedish Occupational Structure, 1950-70

	Agriculture	Industry, etc.	Commerce	Transport & Commerce	Services
1950	20.3	40.8	16.0	8.1	14.8
		A: 22.0%			
1960	13.8	45.1	13.5	7.5	19.8
		W: 78.0%			
		A: 26.8%			
1970	8.1	40.3	12.8	7.2	31.4
		W: 73.2%			

A = administrative employees
W = workers
Source: Compiled by the author.

TABLE 4.4

Trade Unionism Membership, 1957 and 1974
(in thousands)

Federation	1957	1974
Swedish Federation of Trade Unions	1447	1863
Central Organization of Salaried Employees	265	882
Confederation of Professional Organizations	49	115

Source: Compiled by the author.

The Social Democratic links with the trade unions are strong. The workers' trade unions are strong, and practically all those whom they claim to represent are members. Trade union financial support to the Social Democrats is still very important, in spite of lavish public party support, nationally as well as regionally and locally. The trade union contributions emanate both from the membership fees of the numerous members, conveniently delivered through what Swedish terminology calls "collective affiliation," and from special election contributions. The collective affiliation system is the object of constant criticism, especially from the nonsocialist parties but also from many trade unionists, as highly doubtful from a democratic point of view. However, it is too valuable for the Social Democrats to be abandoned, and is defended as less objectionable than industrial contributions to the bourgeois parties. The affiliation system is indicated in Figure 4.2, representing the organizational structure of the Social Democratic Party.

The important point, especially in a comparison with the British system, is that affiliation is decided on the local level, by union branches that decide to affiliate with the local Social Democratic "workers' commune."

Class feelings and struggles are real also in a country with traditionally good labor relations. Their intensity is difficult to estimate, except, possibly, in times of crisis. One measure is, perhaps, the frequency and scope of labor market conflicts. The restless closing years of the 1960s and the early 1970s witnessed far more conflicts than the two previous decades of the postwar era. What exactly the outbursts of industrial unrest indicate is not always clear. It is obvious that many conflicts have been caused primarily by very tangible local problems, related to,

FIGURE 4.2

The Swedish Social Democratic Labour Party Organization

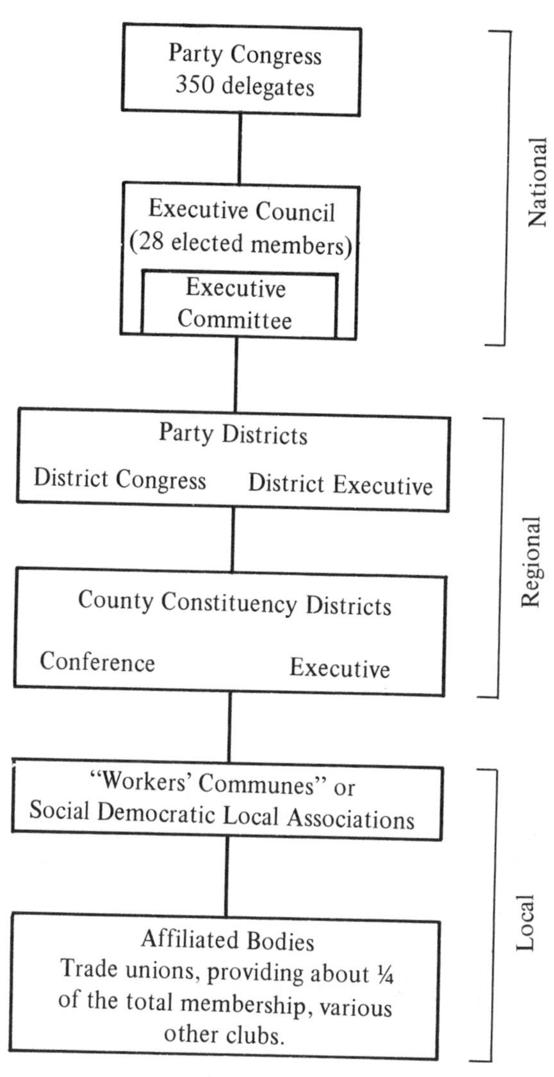

Source: Compiled by the author.

for example, the quality of the physical environment, negotiations on wages and other conditions of work, dismissals, and sometimes to borderline disputes between trade unions claiming the right to negotiate agreements for the same group of employees. The figures in Table 4.5 illustrate the argument.

TABLE 4.5

Stoppages of Work

Year	Stoppages of Work: Total Number	Stoppages of Work: of which Strikes	Number Directly Affected: Employees	Number Directly Affected: Employers	Working Days Lost (000)
1960	31	29	1,479	64	18
1961	12	12	140	12	2
1962	10	10	3,529	10	5
1963	24	23	2,841	31	25
1964	14	14	1,922	14	34
1965	8	8	248	8	4
1966	26	25	29,436	26	352
1967	7	7	90	7	0
1968	7	7	379	7	1
1969	41	40	9,023	36	112
1970	134	134	26,669	211	156
1971	60	59	62,919	161	839
1972	44	44	7,100	37	10
1973	48	48	4,250	41	11
1974	237	237	27,000	219	58

Source: Compiled by the author.

Several important changes have taken place in recent years affecting the relations between the workers and management. They have effected a transfer of (at least) formal power to the workers and their organizations from the management and the owners. Some instances: employee representation on corporation boards, limitations in the right to dismiss employees, right of precedence for labor to interpret collective agreements until the Labour Court has pronounced a verdict on the issue. Add to this that the Swedish Federation of Trade Unions has recently approved a plan for gradual transfer of share ownership in the industries to trade union organizations. This so-called Meidner Plan was a very controversial issue in the Swedish elections on September 19, 1976. The Social Democrats, noting opinion polls adverse both to the plan and to the general concept of "socialism," insisted—in vain—that the question was open and that no decision would be made during the present decade. Industrial spokesmen have maintained that the plan would create difficult problems for Sweden's participation in international industrial integration. Some Social Democratic economists have expressed similar views.

So far, opposition against the development has been surprisingly meek. When the Social Democratic party leader, Olaf Palme, accused the nonsocialist opposition parties of blowing the horn of class struggle,* it was, on the whole, election rhetoric rather than an objective description of facts. The purpose of the accusations was to arouse class loyalty in order to mobilize support from all traditional Social Democratic voters. It is an often-observed fact that Sweden has yet to produce a Glistrup in reaction against high taxes and arbitrary bureaucracy.†

High taxes and transfers are characteristic of the welfare state. The following figures illustrate the Swedish situation in this respect. In 1973 the total national income was estimated at 196,203 million Sw. Cr. Total taxation was 80,749 million Sw. Cr., of which the share of the national government was 52,852 million Sw. Cr. Private consumption amounted to 114,940 million Sw. Cr. Transfers from the national budget to private individuals amount to 31.5 percent of this budget.[3] The tax increases have been accompanied by a dramatic equalization of income retained after taxation and/or, as the case may be, after transfers of various benefits—and also by an almost equally dramatic expansion of the national tax inspection establishment.

HOW EUROPEAN?

Ideologically, culturally, and economically the Swedes regard themselves definitely as "European," in fact as "West European." Measured by the composition of the population, Sweden has become more "all-European" than ever before—or at least since the medieval

*In reply to warnings from the Moderates and the Centre Party that socialism and democracy were irreconcilable.

†Mogens Glistrup, founder and leader of the Danish "Progressive" Party, based on discontent rather than on a clear-cut alternative to the policies of the "traditional" parties.

heyday of the Hanse. Some 10 percent of the population are immigrants, almost half their number come from other countries than Sweden's immediate neighbors. Gradually the immigrants acquire Swedish citizenship if they decide to remain.

Historically the Swedish Social Democrats have old European connections. Social Democracy was "imported" into Sweden from Germany via Denmark. The German influence was very strong in the first decades after the formation of the party in 1889. Its first propaganda activities were in fact based on the German Gotha Programme of 1875. It was followed by a more "national" program in 1897, strongly influenced, however, by the German Erfurt program. Later, influences from Britain could also be observed. The First World War led to conflicts between the German connections and democratic loyalties (also in a neutral country). Between the wars Keynesian economics and the economic policies of the Swedish Social Democrats to meet the economic crisis had much in common. In more recent years the old continental ties were revived through the refugee-generation of German and Austrian Social Democrats (Brandt, Wehner, Kreisky, and others). By that time a successful domestic development as well as an unprecedented tenure of power in a Western democracy had transformed Swedish social democracy into a controversial model, to admire or detest, to reject or to copy—or to do neither.

As the Swedish Social Democrats have held office during, practically speaking, the whole period of "European integration" it is reasonable to assume that the relations of the Social Democrats to Europe, to European integration, and to Atlantic security are identical with those of the Swedish Government. Sweden has, under a Social Democratic Government, joined all European organizations that have been regarded as compatible with her policy for neutrality. At the same time the Swedish Social Democratic leadership looked with considerable suspicion on the European movement, especially during periods dominated by Christian Democrats in Italy and the German Federal Republic, by Gaullists in France, and by Tories in Britain. The suspicion remains, as evidenced in a recent election address by Palme in which he blamed the Swedish opposition for identifying itself with ideas held by European Conservatives.[4]

The ideas of the Social Democrats in relation to European integration were already spelled out in 1961 in a speech by the then Prime Minister Erlander. The theme was Sweden's attitude to the EEC, but in fact also to European and Atlantic integration. It must be remembered that the speech was not a rejection of Europe, only of one specific form of association with the EEC, namely full membership. The necessity of the best possible relations with Europe has always been an axiom for politicians responsible for Swedish affairs, irrespective of party. The argument has concerned how "close, stable and permanent" these relations could be

TABLE 4.6

Sweden's Trade with EEC and EFTA, 1960-75

Year	Imports from	Exports to
	EEC and EFTA Countries	
1960	64.1%	66.1%
1965	70.0	73.7
1970	71.7	72.2
1975	67.9	66.9

Source: Sveriges Offentliga Statistik, Utrikeshandel, II (1965, 1970) and *EFTA Bulletin*, vol. XVII, 1976:6 (1975).

without undermining the credibility of Sweden's dependence on Europe and can be illustrated by the figures in Table 4.6 showing Sweden's trade with EEC and EFTA (European Free Trade Association).

The actions of the Social Democratic Government must be understood against the background of ideological doubts of the kind already referred to, the fact that both Conservatives ("moderates") and Liberals argued in favor of making more serious attempts to investigate the possibilities of reconciling Swedish nonalignment in relation to the power blocs with full membership, and their more immediate responsibility for national security.

When Erlander outlined the Social Democratic and the Swedish position to the Common Market in 1961, association only was regarded as compatible with Sweden's foreign policy.

> The main theme in his speech was the absolute primacy of the nonaligned policy for Swedish foreign policy. This policy had brought the country and its neighbours several advantages. It had also been a positive asset for decreasing international tension and for the work in international organizations where Sweden, thanks to its uncommitted position, had been able to make useful contributions. Also for Sweden's relations with the underdeveloped countries or the new states the policy of neutrality was an asset.
>
> In order to enable Sweden to provide for its own interests in foreign affairs as widely as possible it was necessary to safeguard "a certain degree of freedom of movement both in practice and as laid down by formal agreements." Sweden's nonaligned policy played an important part towards safeguarding this freedom of action, but it had to be supplemented by a consistent effort towards avoiding commitments outside the military realm which might make it difficult or

> impossible for Sweden to choose a neutral course, when confronted with a conflict, and which could make the outside world lose its confidence in Sweden's real desire to select such a political course.
>
> The danger involved in affiliation with the EEC was hence not that the policy of nonalignment would be impossible but rather that it would be inefficient as an instrument of Swedish foreign policy. In order to be efficient in war time, Sweden had to avoid incorporation in the economic system of states who were members in great-power blocs. In order to function at all, the nonaligned policy had to be credible. If this was not so, Sweden could run the danger of an attack from states which believed that the country had in actual fact committed itself to the other side. If the nonaligned position ceased to be credible, the possibilities of Sweden to play a useful international role would be weakened. The different ways in which full membership of the Common Market was thought to bring about unacceptable foreign commitments for Sweden were presented in the speech referred to by the Prime Minister at the Metal Workers' conference in 1961.
>
> The Prime Minister also declared that Sweden was "extremely dubious about entering into an international agreement which would mean that our tariff wall would be raised considerably and, as might be the view of other parts of the world, might lead to the creation of a protectionist trading bloc of prosperous and highly industrialized countries directed against other countries less fortunately placed." This hesitation on the part of the Swedish Government should be understood against the background both of the expanding Swedish assistance to developing countries and to the change in the international power balance which could be foreseen in the future and which has, as a matter of fact, in part already been realized, particularly in the United Nations.[5]

The rest is contemporary history. When, at long last, Britain was deemed worthy of membership and hesitatingly declared herself ready for it, the other EFTA countries had to make up their minds about their future relations with the Common Market. Very much on the basis of the same arguments as those presented by Erlander, the Social Democratic Government decided that no formal membership was possible. However, the decision was made after a long period of hesitation, indicated by the character of the Swedish application for negotiations with the Common Market. The Swedish idea was to find out during the negotiations which form of connection Sweden could accept in view of her basic international position. In March 1971 the Swedish Government issued a declaration explaining the Swedish position:

> Free trade long ago became a fundament line in Swedish policy.
>
> It is in Sweden's interest to take an active part in international economic cooperation aimed at, for instance, the dismantling of tariffs

and other barriers to trade. Our fixity of purpose found expressions in our Brussels declaration on 10th November last year. We there stated that we want to have as close, comprehensive, and durable economic relations with the European Economic Communities as is possible with regard to our neutrality. There has been no change in our position.

We stated, as far back as 10th November, that we considered that there was less likelihood of Sweden becoming a member. Developments since then have borne this out, leading us to the conclusion that in view of our policy of neutrality membership in the EEC is not a realistic possibility for Sweden's part. Since the declaration two essential points have been cleared up.

Participation by Sweden in the foreign-policy cooperation which had been drawn up on the basis of the Davignon report is not compatible with a policy of unwavering Swedish neutrality. EEC membership presupposes participation in this cooperation and acceptance of the political objectives which lie behind it.

By a decision of the Council of Ministers that is based on the Werner Plan, the Community is to be enlarged into an economic and monetary union.

Membership by Sweden in such a union, which would mean that important areas of our national right to self-determination would have to be given up, cannot be compatible with Swedish neutrality.

The Government considers that it is important for our attitude now to be made quite clear. Our preparations and those of the EEC for the subsequent talks can in this way be concentrated on the most essential factual issues. People at home also justifiably require to be informed as soon as possible of the Government's attitude.

We must now concentrate in our contracts with the Communities on attaining as wide cooperation as possible, with due regard to our neutrality. For our part we have proposed, among other things, a customs union comprising both industrial and agricultural products. The form of cooperation should be a special agreement in which the rights and obligations of the parties should be clearly indicated. We must negotiate on such matters. As Sweden will not be included in the EEC Council of Ministers or Commission, special organizational forms of cooperation must be sought that are in keeping with the scope and nature of our collaboration.[6]

This chapter has primarily dealt with the views of the Social Democrats in office on Sweden's possible role in the emerging process of European integration and particularly with the Swedish relations to the Common Market. Several important questions have been left unexplored. These include, inter alia:

1. To what extent were domestic opinions, especially on the left wing of the Social Democratic Party, a decisive force acting against a fuller

Swedish participation in the EEC? My conclusion, so far, is that it was probably more important for the timing than for the content of the decision.

2. The Swedish Social Democrats have been active in collaboration between European Social Democratic parties. Two instances: The action in support of the Portuguese Socialists immediately after the conclusion of the Helsinki CSCE (Conference on Security and Cooperation in Europe); in Palme's Skövde speech that the "Social Democrats of Europe" should work for a UN decision with coercive force to stop all export of arms to and military collaboration with South Africa. In this context Palme made a reference to previous actions in relation both to Greece and to Portugal.

3. The instances may be regarded as illustrating measures to combine European politics both in support of Democratic Socialism against Communism (as well as against a counterrevolution from the right) and in relation to the Third World. As already indicated in Erlander's 1961 speech, consideration for the underdeveloped countries has been one element in the basis for Swedish decisions in relation to the EEC, or at least in the official motives given for them.

4. Which factors existing inside the Social Democratic Party may effect changes in its attitude to Europe? The basic answer is outside factors are likely to be far more important than internal considerations.

5. Will the change of Government shed further light on the European policies of the Social Democrats by effecting significant changes in Swedish policy? Again the answer is negative. Basically the Swedish European policy is a multiparty policy. Swedish business has accepted that it is possible to live—and probably also to thrive—without being participants in the quarrels and decisions in Brussels. But a change of style, with far less of Palmean aggressiveness, is already a fact. The new Swedish foreign minister, Mrs. Soder, immediately after her appointment expressed her belief in speaking softly and firmly.

6. Is it considerations based on specific Social Democratic views of Europe and the world rather than ideas held in common with other major groups in Sweden that are important for the Social Democratic attitude towards the future development of the Swedish defense? The answer is probably both yes and no. All parties are tempered in their defense ambitions by the financial arguments in favor of restricting defense expenditure. In general, the present coalition parties have favored somewhat, but not much, higher defense expenditures than favored by the Social Democrats. This attitude was reflected in the defense budget passed in May 1977; however, the differences between the Government coalition and the majority among the opposition was very small (less than 3 percent).

The Social Democrats are in fact very split on defense. Holding office has, for a long time, had a disciplining effect on left-wing ambitions to effect very substantial reductions of the defense expenditures and of the defense establishment. There are various interests in the Social Democratic Party in relation to defense: outright "old-fashioned" pacifists, romantics dreaming of the Vietnamese or Yugoslav "guerrilla model," people critical of the military as an establishment in the society, and so on. On the whole, however, between the parties as a whole, it has not been a matter of why or if, but rather of how much is enough. Even if the then Minister of Finance, G. E. Strang (68) very likely is on his way out of active politics, his declaration in the 1976 parliamentary debate on defense expenditure is likely to be representative of official Social Democracy, at least while in office:

> Is it necessary to spend 11,150 million kronor on defense?—My answer is that in spite of all disarmament conferences and grandiose security conferences the image of the world is one in which nations are well armed and in some respects increasing their armaments. As an independent, sovereign and neutral nation we must not in this world of cold realities deteriorate our defense strength.

NOTES

1. Tables 4.1 and 4.2 are based on opinion polls at the time of the elections during the years referred to. See *Allmanna valen 1973*, published by the Swedish National Central Bureau of Statistics, pp. 90–91.
2. *Allmanna valen 1973*, table 23, p. 76.
3. *Statistical Abstracts of Sweden*, 1975, pp. 344, 366, 382.
4. Address at the town of Skövde at the annual conference of the Christian Social Democrats (*Broderskapsrörelsen* or "Movement of the Brethren"). The targets for criticism were primarily the Conservatives but also the Centre Party.
5. The analysis of Erlander's speech is quoted from Nils Andrén, *Power-Balance and Non-Alignment* (Uppsala, Sweden: Almqvist & Wiksell, 1967), pp. 119–20.
6. The quoted passages are taken from a speech by Palme at the Stockholm Labour Union, in which he presented the contents of the declaration. *Documents of Swedish Foreign Policy*, 1971, p. 19.

CHAPTER

5

SOCIALIST PARTIES IN NORWAY AND THEIR FOREIGN POLICY POSITIONS

Martin Saeter

INTRODUCTION

Some General Remarks

Three parallel and partly interlinked processes seem at present to be contributing to the need of a general reassessment of the role of ideology in the European context: detente, West European integration, and the rise to power of communist parties in some West European countries.

As long as the East-West confrontation was regarded as nearly identical with the ideological division between communism and democracy, communism and left-wing socialism in Western Europe were regarded as an extension of Soviet influence. In this sense, ideology became part of the overall balance of power in Europe. The cold war accentuated the ideological differences and blurred the lines between ideology and power politics.

To some extent the policy of detente has reversed this trend, among other things by contributing to a separation of power politics from ideology (cf. "peaceful coexistence") and by making ideological differences within the blocs more visible. However, as long as the general balance of power in Europe rested entirely on the policies of the two superpowers whose ideologies remain diametrically opposed, the effect of detente in this respect could but remain limited.

The development of the EC into a stronger and more independent political entity introduced a potential for change in the East-West situation in Europe, both at the ideological level and at the level of balance-of-power politics. What the EC gained in strength, would not necessarily be at the expense of the Soviet Union or to the benefit of the United States. Combined with the policy of detente, the development of the EC could prove to be the balancing force needed to allow for a dismantling of blocs in Europe.

The increased strength and the ideological as well as political development of the communist parties in "Latin Europe," especially the French and Italian ones, have brought a further dimension to East-West developments in Europe. The crucial question is, of course, the relations of the West European communist parties with Moscow. The accession to governmental power of communist parties loyal to Moscow in big countries like France and Italy would be likely to upset the general East-West balance and to have serious repercussions on the superpower relationship.

The declaration by the leading West European communist parties of their independence from Moscow and the confirmation of this principle of independence by the communist summit meeting in East Berlin in June 1976 might therefore be interpreted as a realistic adjustment to a continued process of detente and to the requirements of a further political integration in the EC.

Built into this situation, there seems to be a peculiar self-reinforcing give-and-take logic: To the extent that Moscow wants to realize its aim of an all-European system of security and cooperation, implying a reduced U.S. military posture in Europe, it will have to accept the development of an independent EC. An independent EC, however, is incompatible with the rise to governmental power of strong Moscow-led communist parties in the great EC countries.

The willingness of the Italian and French communists to accept the existing political framework, including the EC, as a basis for their future political activity seems to be part of this reassessment.

The Relevance of the Theme

Against the background of these East-West developments in Europe, the ideologies and political profiles of the socialist parties in countries like Norway and Denmark become of general interest, because these countries are, and will remain, parts of the overall European picture. It is therefore relevant to submit their ideological developments to the same kind of investigation, to the same questions, as in the case of the greater West European countries. Among the questions to be dealt with are the following ones:

- How do the parties in question define socialism?
- How do they conceive the transition to socialism?

• What changes does such a transition imply?

• Do they accept working for socialism through existing political institutions?

• What is their attitude towards parliamentary democracy?

• Do they still adhere to the doctrines of democratic centralism, dictatorship of the proletariat, proletarian internationalism, and, if so, in what sense?

• What are their attitudes towards Moscow?

• Are their primary loyalties to their own nations or to the international socialist or communist "movement"?

• Will their accession to political power be likely to increase Soviet influence in their own countries?

• How do they look upon European integration?

• Do they reject the EC, and, if so, on what premises?

• What is their attitude towards NATO?

• And to the United States?

• What are the possible implications of their participation in government for Atlantic relations?

These and similar questions will be dealt with on the following pages. The study will concentrate on the main Norwegian socialist parties, the Communists, the Left Socialists, and the social democratic Labour Party. First, however, there is a general overview of the Norwegian voters' party orientations.

Party Preferences Among Norwegian Voters

According to "Gallup's political barometer" (Norges Markedsdata A/S), the socialist parties taken together have gained in strength since the last general election (1973), receiving, at the beginning of 1977, support from more than 50 percent of the voters. Within the socialist camp there has been, over the last two years, a strong upward trend for the Labour Party (DNA) and a downward trend for the Socialist Left Party (SV). Table 5.1 shows the party preferences of those who stated their intention to vote.

Party Titles and Abbreviations

AIK: Arbeidernes Informasjonskomite (The Workers' Information Committee)

AKP (m-l): Arbeidernes Kommunistiske Parti (Workers' Communist Party, Marxist-Leninist)

TABLE 5.1

Stated Party Preferences of Norwegian Voters

Election	Det norske Arbeiderparti (DNA) The Norwegian Labour Party	Fremskrittspartiet (Frp) The Progressive Party	Det nye Folkepartiet (DnF) The New People's Party	Høyre (H) The Conservative Party	Kristelig Folkeparti (Kr.F) The Christian Democratic Party	Senterpartiet (SP) The Center Party	Sosialistisk Venstreparti (SV) Socialist Left Party	Venstre (V) The Liberal Party	Andre Others
1973	35.3	5.0	3.4	17.4	12.2	11.0	11.2	3.5	1.0
May 1975	31.9	2.9	3.4	21.3	13.5	12.5	10.2	2.5	1.0
Sept. 1975	37.5	1.6	3.6	21.3	13.9	10.6	6.8	3.2	0.8
Jan. 1976	39.6	1.0	2.1	22.4	11.2	12.3	7.1	3.4	0.3
Sept. 1976	44.9	0.9	1.4	21.0	11.0	11.3	5.1	2.5	1.8
New method of assessment:									
Oct. 1976	44.3	0.9	1.5	20.6	11.6	12.6	3.9	2.8	1.9
Mar. 1977	43.7	1.2	2.8	22.0	9.5	9.8	5.5	4.2	1.8

Source: Aftenposten, 14 April 1977.

DNA: Det norske Arbeiderparti (The Norwegian Labour Party)
NKP: Norges Kommunistiske Parti (The Communist Party of Norway)
SF: Sosialistisk Folkeparti (Socialist People's Party)
SV: Sosialistisk Venstreparti (Socialist Left Party)

THE NORWEGIAN LABOUR PARTY (DET NORSKE ARBEIDERPARTI—DNA)

To discuss the domestic and foreign policy line of the Norwegian Labour Party (DNA) is to discuss what has been the mainstream of Norwegian politics since the Second World War. Except for a couple of breaks in the 1960s and the beginning of the 1970s, DNA has formed the government for all the time, having had an absolute majority in the Storting until 1961. At the general elections of 1973—after the EC referendum—its number of seats in the Storting was reduced from 74 to 62 (of 155), representing some 35 percent of the votes. But since there was a socialist majority—the Socialist Electoral Alliance (SV) got 16 seats—there was, in practice, no bourgeois alternative, and DNA formed a minority government that still remains in power. In the Gallup polls, DNA reached its lowest ebb in the spring of 1975, receiving support from less than 32 percent of the voters. Since then the trend has turned; March 1977 polls show that more than 43 percent of the voters would vote DNA. Having for a long time been a majority party and a governing party at that, DNA has in practice had the opportunity to answer all the questions that are now being presented to communist and socialist parties in Southern Europe. Like its sister parties in Denmark, Sweden, Austria, the Federal Republic of Germany, and others, it has made sufficiently clear that it is no revolutionary party, that it accepts and seeks change only through gradual reforms and on the basis of a majority consent; also that, in government position, it remains loyal to international commitments, including NATO, and so forth.

Given the dominating position of DNA in Norwegian politics during the last decades, it makes little sense to discuss its "socialist" foundation as something incalculable, as something that might change Norwegian relations to the rest of Europe or even European relations to the United States. DNA is the main architect of Norwegian foreign policy since the war. As to NATO membership and the policy of alliance in general, there has been, all the time, a solid consensus between DNA and the bourgeois parties, in spite of some dissidents on the left wing. However, as already mentioned, on the question of membership in the EC, DNA was severely split, but so were other Norwegian parties. This traumatic event in Norwegian politics was much too complex to be reduced to a question of socialism versus liberalism (or conservatism).

Recent research analyses and public opinion polls have shown that the changes in attitudes toward the EC differ markedly from those determining the attitudes towards NATO. There has also been a notable swing of opinions over the last years. While NATO support has increased, the percentage of those favoring Norwegian membership in the EC has declined dramatically. In 1973 the incongruency between NATO attitudes and EC attitudes made itself most strongly felt in the center of the party spectrum. Of "moderate" voters at that time, as many as 91 percent supported NATO membership, while only 42 percent of the same voters were in favor of Norwegian membership in the EC. "Radicals" as well as "conservatives" showed more congruency in their attitudes, but even among those groups the percentage favoring NATO exceeded that favoring EC by 30. Among DNA voters, the percentage supporting NATO rose from 70 to 88 in the period 1965–73.[1]

Results of the April 1977 poll[2] presented in Table 5.2 show a very low percentage in favor of EC membership over the whole party spectrum, increasing the incongruency between EC and NATO attitudes still more (14 to 86). An exception is the SV, whose high percentage of anti-NATO voters mujst be seen with the background that this party has now been strongly reduced numerically, so that the "hard-core" attitudes dominate.

The almost astonishingly low percentage in support of EC membership probably reflects a general acceptance of the Government's view that the 1973 referendum settled this question for the foreseeable future.

In the EC question, the Norwegian Labour Party split on the grounds of ideology as well as on differences of economic and other interests. Urban radicals tended to oppose EC membership, and so did smallholders and fishers, a large number of whom traditionally voted DNA. Unlike Denmark, where Copenhagen was more against EC membership than the rest of the country, the center-periphery dimension made itself strongly felt in Norway in the sense that the capital and central districts around Oslo were generally more pro-EC than other parts of the country.[3]

Although the policy of the DNA leadership was explicitly in favor of Norwegian membership in the EC, the party line since the referendum has been one of strict observation of the decision taken by the majority of the people: that the relations to the EC should be based on the trade treaty. This line has contributed considerably to the healing of the wounds from the campaign inside the party. It is difficult to imagine that the DNA government will risk reopening them by a new membership initiative. On

TABLE 5.2

Attitudes toward Membership in NATO and EC by Party Affiliation

Continued Membership in NATO	(Total)	Labor (DNA)	Sos. Left (SV)	Cons. (H)	Chr. Dem. Kr.F)	Center (SP)	Others
Yes	86	92	12	93	94	92	78
No	10	3	83	3	4	2	17
DK	4	5	4	2	2	4	4
OA	–	–	–	2	–	–	–
NA	–	–	–	1	–	2	–
Given a new EC referendum tomorrow, how would you vote?							
Yes	14	18	–	21	16	–	19
No	58	52	100	49	64	86	71
Refuse	2	4	–	2	2	2	2
DK and NA	25	26	–	27	19	12	8

Source: Norges Markedsdata A/S/, ordre nr. 018Y/77, April 1, 1977.

the other hand, the result of the referendum has to some degree put an end to the consensus formerly existing between the Conservatives and DNA in the question of Norway's policy towards Europe. Also, in other fields of foreign policy the cleavage between DNA and the Conservatives seems to be widening, apparently not so much because of any change in the government's attitudes as because of the changed situation itself. This requires adjustments and adaptation, and the opposition party would like the government to adjust and adapt in a way different from what it is doing. In the following sections we will return to some of the concrete questions on which disagreements exist. Suffice it to say here that these differences are not so much of an ideological nature as concerned with the overall political struggle for power and influence in the Norwegian society where, of course, ideology is part of the picture. We now turn to the question of the official ideological profile of DNA. As mentioned above, there is no reason to believe that social democratic ideology will now suddenly start changing Norwegian politics. On the contrary, there is every reason to expect continuity in Norwegian politics on the basis of that ideology. This expectation of a stable development is perhaps what makes the politics of the Scandinavian social democratic parties of interest to other Europeans too.

Ideology

The first paragraph of DNA's "Principles and Perspectives," adopted in 1969, reads as follows:

> The aims of the Norwegian Labour Party are those of a *socialist society*. This will be a society in which democracy prevails in every field, where there is equality among all people and groups, with the greatest possible liberty for the individual as long as he does not hurt others. To attain these aims and to safeguard the individual, the people in common will have to direct the development. This aim is international. Together with persons of the same opinion in other countries we will struggle for the realization of the ideas of democratic socialism.

Although DNA is a mass party comprising people of different opinions and interests in many respects, there seems to be a broad agreement within the party about the main principles of democratic socialism. It is conceived and presented as a clearly reformist strategy, as an alternative, a "third way," distinct from totalitarian communism as well as from liberal capitalism. It is more a concept of government as a political *process* than a vision of a future perfect society. The party chairman, Reiulf Steen, says it this way:

> Democratic socialism builds on a concept of society which regards economic, social, and cultural development as a process in which the labour movement considers its primary task as being to adopt as its own the needs and opinions of the broad popular masses and then to articulate the criticism and turn it into constructive reforms.[4]

According to Steen, each new generation of democratic socialists will have to define its own concrete aims, but the *direction* is given, pointing toward a more *human society*. The ideal is a society in which man stands in a productive relationship to other men and to nature and "is rich, not because of what he *owns*, but (because of) what he *is*." The dominance of the forces of capital exercised through the established power structures hinders, however, the liberation of the individual and his possibilities of realizing himself.[5]

Steen acknowledges his debt to Marxist thought of the kind Marx himself developed after 1850. But he strongly rejects the Leninist version, the dictatorship of the proletariat and the democratic centralism:

> The attempts by Lenin and other prominent Soviet communists at developing Marxism opened the way for the most horrible crimes in the name of socialism. . . . Democratic centralism turns into totalitarian centralism and the dictatorship of the proletariat easily develops into the dictatorship of the party organs and party bosses.[6]

The DNA leadership wants to distinguish the party clearly from any kind of totalitarian ideology. The image of DNA is one of a welfare-oriented pragmatism. "The role of ideology is to sum up the insights we have gained into the society in which we live, and on this basis to draw the policy lines for the future."[7]

The social democratic DNA has been accused by the Socialist Left Party of having developed into "an effective administrator of capitalism."[8] In explaining the difference between bourgeois democracy and democratic socialism Steen underlines the role of labor organizations. Democratic socialism, according to him, is not merely an extension of bourgeois democracy into ever more sectors of public life even if this might be important enough in itself. One must, in addition, "utilize the sources of being together and living together such as we find in the labour movement itself."[9] "A strong and rich organizational activity in the trade unions and the other great organizations of the labour movement constitutes the fundamental basis for new drives towards democracy," Steen maintains, adding that this means that the organizations must be endowed with real powers in the sense that they also "formulate the policy."[10] This increased role of labor organizations is in a long-term perspective apparently regarded as a very important matter by the DNA leadership. Among the organizations, the LO (Landsorganisjonen) is by far the most important one. It has always been closely related to DNA and led centrally by DNA people. However, the local influence of NKP, SV and even AKP (m-1) members is strong in many places. There are often bitter conflicts between the latter and DNA. The DNA leadership has made it clear that ideologically there can be no question of a compromise either with the NKP or with the AKP (m-1). As Reiulf Steen sees it, a cleavage based on a clear, ideological difference is nothing to deplore. It is a necessity. "However, a cleavage springing from disagreement on particular, practical questions, not to speak of . . . personal conflicts, is disastrous, causing a weakening of the working possibilities for the whole labour movement."[11]

It will probably turn out to be difficult for the parties in question to differentiate between ideological and practical questions in accordance with Steen's view. How great the difficulties will be, depends to a large extent on the general political climate at the domestic as well as on the international level.

In the trade unions, the NKP seems to be creating less trouble for DNA than the two other parties mentioned. Ideologically, DNA and NKP are too widely apart really to be rivals, and, as mentioned elsewhere in this study, at the practical level the communists are bent on cooperation with DNA. In addition, they constitute just a tiny minority. As to the AKP (m-1), there can be no reconciliation whatsoever, at either level. In spite of their rather insignificant numbers, the AKP members are conducting considerable propaganda inside certain key industries, using methods aimed at stirring up feelings. On the other hand, the conflict with these radical forces has the effect of giving DNA a profile of stability and responsibility dear to the ordinary worker.

The real challenge to DNA in the trade unions is the Socialist Left Party. Similarity of ideology as well as of interest often makes it difficult to draw a dividing line between the two parties. As shown by the polls since the EC campaign, a large number of left-wing social democrats have been fluctuating between DNA and SV. It seems to be equally clear that large-scale defections of social democrats take place only in connection with issues that really divide the nation and then as a protest against the policy of the DNA government on these specific issues.

The conclusion seems warranted that the outcome of the rivalry between DNA and SV in the trade unions, as well as at the general national level, will depend above all on the ability of the Labour government to avoid critical national issues of such a divisive nature. As a party with a "majority ideology" and taking care of "national interests," DNA, in such conflicts, becomes vulnerable to attacks from the left, especially in the field of foreign policy. In this respect, the massive return of social democrats to DNA from the SV during the last year is an indication that the policy line of the government in crucial areas has been successful. DNA seems to have profited from the general policy of detente, which makes questions related to security and alliance policy less controversial. The government's oil and energy policy, which in some quarters is regarded as somewhat "nationalistic," no doubt strongly contributes to pacifying the left-wing social democrats. So also does the active and progressive attitude taken by the government in relation to the demands of the developing countries. In addition, the sharpened quarrel between DNA and the Conservatives because of the government's policy of gradual socialization of key industries, reduces the weight of the SV argument that the DNA government is only an administrator of the capitalist system.

NATO and Europe

In the fields of Atlantic security and European integration, DNA is pursuing a policy of continuity. In its "working programme 1974–1977" the party states as its aim that Norway should base her security on continued membership in NATO and, within this framework, work actively for detente, arms control, and disarmament. The policy concerning bases as well as nuclear weapons should remain unchanged. This is a line that is firmly supported by a majority in the party as well as in the nation in general.

Traditionally, and in accordance with the dominant trend in Norwegian debate, DNA has tended to regard Atlantic security and European cooperation as much the same thing. The above-mentioned program, however, explicitly differentiates between various aspects of European and Atlantic relations, showing a willingness to reconsider the policy in light of the progress of detente. In this context, the prospect of a possible all-European security system receives considerable attention:

> The Western defense cooperation was never intended to be a permanent solution to the problems of security, and it is therefore necessary to maintain Norwegian security policy under permanent review in order to obtain the most servicable solutions. In the present phase, the effort to establish an all-European security arrangement is in the foreground. Norway should regard this as an important step in the striving for a global security system.

As for the question of European integration, this is regarded as settled, in the sense that the relations between Norway and the EC are to be based on the results of the referendum of 1972, that is, on the basis of the trade treaty. This does not mean, however, that Norway should abstain from taking part in the shaping of European politics. On the contrary, Norway should also in future "actively engage in strengthening cooperation with the countries of Western Europe." DNA itself attaches great importance to cooperation with related parties and labor organizations in other European countries. In this context, an interesting distinction is made between cooperation within the West European framework on one side and at the all-European level on the other. As to the first distinction the program states:

> The Labour Party has as its aim the establishment of an organized cooperation with persons of the same opinion in Western Europe, especially with the aim of forming a socialist programme for Europe. Special attention has to be given to the realization of democracy and equality in every field of society, a stronger social government, control of multinational companies, the solution of important environmental problems, and of a positive attitude towards the developing countries.

As to the second—the all-European aspect—the stress is more on cooperation between countries. The statement reflects the ambitious vision of a social democratic "Europe":

> The Labour Party aims at establishing a close cooperation between the trade union and political labour movements of the European countries, which can constitute the basis for a democratic socialist policy for Europe. Every possibility must be used to increase the contacts and cooperation between East and West in Europe.

Like their fellow social democrats in the other Scandinavian countries, the Norwegian social democrats have taken great interest in the ideological developments in the left-wing parties of Southern Europe. The main party organ, "Arbeiderbladet," reflects the general attitude of DNA when commenting on the abandonment of totalitarianism and the acceptance of democratic rules of the game by the Italian and French communist parties:

> We interpret these signals as an expression of the fact that ideologically these parties have capitulated. . . . This is positive. . . . If communist parties have a strong popular backing and accepting democratic rules of the game participate in West European governments, this is in itself no disaster. . . . rather a *challenge*.[12]

The party chairman, Reiulf Steen, draws a general conclusion from developments in these South European parties, which implicitly relates to the situation of social democratic mass parties in any country:

> Parties obtaining support from more than 35 percent of the voters have to choose between continued progress, meaning abandonment of dogmatic attitudes (on the one hand), and sticking to these (attitudes), experiencing setbacks (on the other). . . . The size and political reality bring you into what was formerly called revisionism . . . but what is political realism.[13]

Mr. Kissinger's warnings about the possible consequences of a communist participation in West European governments were in general commented upon negatively by most of the Norwegian press. The DNA chairman rejected them outright as incompatible with the role of the Atlantic alliance:

> The basic purpose of participating in a defence alliance is in my opinion to prevent, if necessary by military means, foreign forces from intervening in the development of the nation. . . . One might put a huge question mark over the function of NATO if the purpose of alliance were to be extended to include the internal affairs of a country, as long as that country's political course is decided through free elections.[14]

THE SOCIALIST LEFT PARTY (SOSIALISTISK VENSTREPARTI—SV)

The plan to unite the Socialist People's Party (SF), the Worker's Information Committee (AIK) and the Communist Party of Norway into a single party was put forward by SF in 1973. It was meant as a continuation of the already successful cooperation, first in the "People's Movement Against Norwegian Membership of the EC" and thereafter in the Socialist Election Alliance. The idea was that the new party, the Socialist Left Party (SV) should be the only Marxist party to the left of the Labour Party. There was a strong pressure from the SF to have the existing party organizations dissolved as soon as possible and to replace them by new commonly and democratically elected leadership organs.

As could have been expected, the reservations against this line were strongest in the NKP, which preferred to retain the looser form of alliance between three formally separate parties. The NKP Congress in March 1974 nevertheless decided to accept the demand for a dissolution of the party, provided that the negotiations that were to start between the parties led to agreement about the future basis of cooperation. This turned out to be a highly controversial decision inside the NKP. The debate within the communist party as well as the negotiations between the parties revealed fundamental differences on several questions. The NKP demanded that the new party should build on Marxism-Leninism and that there must be an agreement beforehand on strategy and tactics for a step-by-step transformation of society to socialism. Furthermore, the new party should aim for a broad alliance of the Left and the uniting of "the people's democratic forces" that would take the lead in the "anti-monopolistic struggle." Last, but not least, the party should build on "proletarian internationalism."

In the negotiations before and during the Founding Congress in Trondheim, March 1975, there turned out to be three main themes of disagreement: the party's program, its attitude towards the socialist countries, and the merger progress.

Because of the NKP's refusal to accept decisions on such fundamental questions taken by majority voting, the following main issues were not settled at the congress, but were postponed for later discussions and decisions:[15]

1) the SV's relation to Marxism-Leninism,
2) tactics and strategy,
3) the analysis of state monopoly capitalism,
4) proletarian internationalism.

The NKP accepted, despite strong internal disagreements, to continue the process of merger, reserving the right for the party's highest organ, the congress, to take the final decision at its meetings scheduled for the autumn. However, there were still strong objections inside the NKP to the SF's request that the SV congress, in its "Programme of Principles" explicitly condemn the Soviet intervention in Czechoslovakia in 1968 and express its critical attitude to developments in the socialist countries. But NKP opposition could not hinder the congress adopting a declaration referring to a former statement condemning the "serious violations of fundamental socialist principles" that had taken place during the Stalin era, and criticizing the continued absence in the Soviet Union of "rights for which socialists in Norway have always struggled and on which they will build further in their work for socialism in our country." As for its reference to Czechoslovakia, communist opposition was evaded by drawing attention to a paragraph in the previously agreed program of principles. This paragraph runs as follows:

> The relations between socialist states must build on respect for the independence and sovereignty of every country, and on equality and noninterference in internal affairs. Any violation of these principles is

> detrimental to socialism. Any use of force against other countries which violates the right of the people to decide its own development must be condemned.

Against the background of these differences the NKP congress decided in the autumn of 1975 that the NKP should continue as an independent party on its own ideological and political basis. A significant minority, including the deposed chairman, Reidar T. Larsen, opposed this decision, staying in the new SV party.

The Socialist Left Party (SV) was intended by its founders to become the only Marxist party to the left of the social democratic Labour Party. It presented itself as a radical alternative to the latter. Ideologically, it was—and is—a very heterogeneous party, its membership ranging from orthodox revolutionary communists to radical liberals, from atheists to active Christians, from pacifists to supporters of a strong national defense, from city industrial workers to periphery smallholders. What united them all into one party was the feeling created by the anti-EC campaign that one could successfully mobilize against the establishment. The new image of the NKP as a highly respectable partner capable of operating with conservatives and liberals as well as the Christians in the People's Movement[16] contributed to reducing ideological conflicts and benefitted cooperation on practical questions.

The SV has sought to demonstrate unity by taking "radical" stands, opposing the governing Labour Party on concrete political issues. But there obviously is a dilemma: by strongly opposing DNA the SV risks being looked upon as too much of a negative protest party, a risk that is all the greater because in the present parliamentary situation the only credible alternative to the Labour government is a bourgeois government. On the other hand, a close cooperation with DNA might mean a loss of identity and an undermining of the SV's cultivated image as a socialist alternative. This again might invite questions about the justification of maintaining the SV as a separate party. The SV thus becomes vulnerable to both sides. Recent polls are not encouraging: in June 1976 only about 5 percent of the voters supported the SV, compared with more than 10 percent a year earlier.

The SV is, according to the party program, clearly a Marxist, but not a Marxist-Leninist party. The SV regards Marxism not as a dogmatic *Weltanschauung*, but as the basis of historical-materialistic analysis. Norway is looked upon as an increasingly capitalist society in which economic power is concentrated in the hands of ever fewer people, a tendency that is strengthened by the growing dominance of the multinational companies.

SV regards it as one of the party's chief aims to unite the forces of labor against monopoly capitalism. The experiences of the anti-EC struggle is seen as a proof that this is feasible. The SV is consequently in favor of an "action community" in the overall struggle for a socialist society. Organizing the working class becomes, in this perspective, of fundamental importance. Regarding the social democratic Labour Party as having betrayed this goal by cooperating with the capitalistic forces, the SV deems it necessary to fight DNA in the work places. An end must be put to DNA dominance in the LO. Among other things, the practice of collective membership of trade unions in DNA must be abolished.

The SV's attitude towards social democracy is stated in the party program as follows:

> Social democracy furthers economic growth within the framework of capitalism, taking a positive attitude towards big industry and serving the interests of great units at the expense of the small ones. The social democratic dominance within the labour movement is aimed at keeping the class struggle within the framework of capitalism. In this way, the right wing of the labour movement becomes an effective administrator of capitalism. Through class cooperation it pacifies the trade unions, makes initiatives from below difficult, hinders a political and ideological development of the working class.

According to the program, the SV wants to promote a change through reforms, and advocates that the struggle for reforms start on the basis of the existing system. This, however, should not mean cooperation with the enemy, the capitalism of the bourgeois society. To achieve a transition from capitalism to socialism, reforms alone are not sufficient. There will have to be a "unifying strategy" leading "beyond the borders of capitalism":

> a chain of reforms directed against monopoly capitalism as links in a solid strategy can lead to a point where fundamental socialist revolution starts.

The program explicitly states that "Capitalism cannot be abolished gradually through reforms. The transition to socialism requires a radical break with capitalism." It is difficult to get a clear picture of what kind of a radical break this is supposed to be. There is, however, one paragraph in the program that might be interpreted as pointing in the direction of a complete abolishment of the parliamentary system:

> As part of the socialist revolution the working people must establish democratic organs that secure (for them) the power and the control of society. Through these (organs) the people choose and control their leaders and participate in the (process of) management and organization.

This "socialist state power" will abolish the free market economy, free competition, and so on, and undertake a full "socialization."

In the meantime, the SV will struggle for reforms of a more limited nature, thus preparing for the socialist revolution. To such reforms belong the nationalization of foreign investment capital in Norway, of credit institutions, key industries, transport and trade, and so forth.

The SV believes that the ever more far-reaching and pressing global problems present Norway with a challenge that can best be met if Norway retains her full sovereignty and freedom of action. The party is therefore against Norwegian membership in supranational organizations, including the EC and IEA (International Energy Agency). Norway's association with the IEA, for instance, is seen as potentially dangerous in crisis situations because of the close linkage with NATO in the military—and especially the nuclear—field.

The official party attitude is that Norway should withdraw from NATO to regain her sovereignty in the field of military policy, thereby following up the refusal of September 1972 to give up her sovereignty to the EC in the economic and general foreign policy field. NATO is regarded as an alliance of the rich Western World against weaker countries, as well as being an instrument in the rivalry between the two superpowers. It is maintained that far from increasing the security of Norway, it reduces it (by increasing the risk of Norway being drawn into superpower conflicts, not only those arising in Europe, but also elsewhere). Some SV people do admit, however, that the NATO guarantee might to some extent be an effective instrument of deterrence and that a Norwegian withdrawal might have a destabilizing effect on the East-West situation. This is seen to be a result of the rigid situation created more by the alliance policy itself than as a consequence of any previously existing threat from the Soviet Union. However, Norway's NATO membership as such is at present not regarded by the SV elite as a burning question. To judge from the general debate, there is now a willingness in the leadership to consider a *gradual* diminution of alliance functions, starting from a mutually agreed dissolution of the military organizations on both sides in Europe.

However, the predominant view is that Norway should not make her withdrawal from NATO and her transition to neutrality dependent on progress in the East-West negotiations.

The dominant way of reasoning seems to be that neither of the superpowers would risk an overt aggressive military attack on a neutral European country because of the tremendous consequences this could have on the superpower relationship itself and because of the reactions it would be bound to provoke in other parts of the world. By setting an example, Norway could contribute to the dismantling of blocs and to progress towards a real disarmament in Europe. The SV is the party that most strongly criticizes armaments and armament expenditures. Its official attitude is not pacifist. The party wants a reorganization of the defense on a purely national and decentralized basis.

Being strongly opposed to Norwegian membership, as well as to closer relations with the Community in general, the SV has, so to speak, made EC developments a taboo subject in the intraparty discussions. It is therefore difficult to speak of any "party attitudes" toward, for instance, the idea of a "socialist" EC or cooperation between socialist parties on a European basis. Generally speaking, the SV is positive to international cooperation between all socialist and communist parties, without making similarity of ideology a precondition. At present the leadership especially underlines the need to develop active cooperation with other Nordic socialist parties; with West European communist parties, above all those of Italy, France, Spain, and Greece; and with the liberation movements of South Africa, the PLO (Palestine Liberation Organization), the opposition in Chile, and other movements in similar positions.

THE COMMUNIST PARTY OF NORWAY (NKP)

On the basis of the lessons drawn from the period of SV negotiations, the new chairman of the party, Martin Gunnar Knutsen, has declared it to be of primary importance in the time ahead to reconstruct the image of the NKP as an independent party with a clear ideological and theoretical profile.[17] He argues that if the NKP had been integrated into the SV, there would have been no revolutionary Marxist-Leninist party left in Norway except for the "Maoist" Workers' Communist Party (AKP), which he condemns for its "anti-communist" and "anti-Soviet" attitudes.[18] A true Marxist-Leninist party is needed, he claims, both as part of the world communist movement and above all as a leading force in the class struggle of the labor movement in Norway "to present the communist alternative to that of the class cooperation policy as practiced by the labour right-wing leadership."[19]

Starting from the conviction that it is unrealistic to believe that an extension of democracy in the sense of a transfer of power to the working class is possible without class struggle, the NKP sees its role as being to carry out a continuing critique of the existing capitalistic structures of society without compromising its socialist aims. As a Marxist-Leninist party, basing its analysis of society on the philosophy and methods of dialectical historical materialism, the NKP regards itself as being in an avant-garde position, able to undertake such constructive critique on a scientific basis and thus to show the direction in which socialism has to develop. Thereby it intends also to influence the other socialist and left-wing forces, including social democracy. This function seems at present to be the main reason why the party wants to retain the label "Leninist."

The NKP is founded on the principle of democratic centralism: full participation of every member on every level in exercising criticism and self-criticism, democratic majority decisions, acceptance of majority decisions by each member, the right of everyone to fight for his own points of view inside the party framework.

Officially the party fully accepts the existing parliamentary system as a democratic basis on which it must build for the foreseeable future. There is no question of abolishing existing democratic rights, but of "extending" democracy into economic life: "A democratic socialization" must be undertaken to achieve a real transfer of power to the people. All important means of production should be owned by society. A socialized sector of industry has to be given a decisive role in the whole economy. It must be extended to banking and other credit institutions, insurance companies, key industries like petrochemicals, trade and transport, the whole energy sector, and so forth. In these socialized parts of the economy, the workers must be given greater say in management, exercising control through democratically elected bodies.

Fully developed socialism will not appear as soon as capitalism is abolished. The socialist form of society will be under permanent development and change. Because of the different social and economic conditions existing in the different countries, owing to historic, geographical, national, and international factors, the methods of building socialism and the forms of political organization of socialist society will differ from country to country.[20]

The socialist society develops into ever more perfect stages, not automatically, "but through conscious action on the part of the working class and its party, which presumes that the working class and its party have the political power firmly in their hands."[21] "Qualitative changes" have to be introduced at each new stage.

The NKP advocates a peaceful transition to socialism, arguing that this would be in accordance with the traditions of the labor movement in Norway. Several factors favor such a development: The working class has a majority in the nation, and it is well organized. There are few, if any, feudal remnants, no class of landowners, and no military castes.

A peaceful change to socialism is, however, dependent on the condition that "the governing class cannot, or is given no possibility to use direct force against the people."[22]

Norwegian membership in NATO is seen by the party leadership as "a significant negative factor," tying Norway "politically and militarily (not only economically) directly to world imperialism."[23] The struggles for disarmament and for a neutral Norwegian foreign policy are therefore regarded as decisive preconditions for a peaceful transition to socialism. NKP wants "equally good relations" with socialist and capitalist countries in the economic as well as the political and cultural fields. The foreign policy program further includes a nonnuclear zone in the Nordic area; closer Nordic cooperation; good relations with the Soviet Union; support for national liberation movements; increased help to developing countries; replacement of free trade by a system of long-term trade treaties, and so on.

As mentioned earlier, relations with the world communist movement and especially the Soviet Union were the cause of bitter conflict between the NKP and the SV. The NKP defines itself as part of the world communist movement, categorically rejecting the possibility of a "third way" between capitalist imperialism and socialism.[24]

Proletarian internationalism is, however, not to be understood as something opposed to patriotism or even as subservience to Moscow. It is defined as solidarity with the working class in the socialist countries, with the national and social liberation movements and with the sister parties in the capitalist countries or, as Knutsen said at the Berlin conference: "solidarity of workers across international borders."[25] The party chairman strongly underlines that the NKP is "an independent party which in no way is remotely controlled; and in no way a satellite of another communist party." It is a "part of the working class in our country, a democratic, Norwegian party."[26]

At the Berlin conference in June 1976 the NKP chairman seemed to agree with the generally accepted line when he stated "that communists are patriots as well as internationalists."[27] At the same time he very sharply condemned what he observed as strengthened tendencies to "anti-Sovietism" in the Norwegian debate. There is an interesting feature to be noticed in his argumentation on this point. He condemns "anti-Sovietism" not so much on the ground of ideology as on the ground of what he terms national Norwegian interests in the context of power politics:

> It will be an important task for the communists in Norway in the time ahead, together with all progressive forces, to intensify the struggle against any watering down of Norwegian base policy and at the same time to unmask the anti-communism and anti-Sovietism, whatever disguise it may assume. This policy is in accordance with the interests of the whole Norwegian peole, and aims at good relations with all neighbouring countries, including the Soviet Union.[28]

The NKP thus seems to have no difficulty combining endorsement of the idea of an independent national road to socialism with friendly attitude towards the Soviet Union.

To what degree this combination reflects the particular Norwegian geographical and strategic position, it is difficult to assess. Looked at in the national context, this NKP line of friendship towards the Soviet Union is uncontroversial to the extent that ideology can be distinguished from "national interest," inasmuch as it is in accordance with the official Norwegian policy. As long as the climate of detente lasts, there will apparently be no direct reason for conflict between DNA and the NKP in this respect.

At present, the Socialist Left Party seems to have a greater need to criticize the policy of the Labour government as well as the policies of both superpowers in general.

In a European perspective the position of the NKP on this point does not seem very complicated. Given a continued policy of detente, a more independent line by the big West European communist parties towards the CPSU would fit into a more independent role for the EC as a whole in the East-West context. However, as long as Norway is not a member of EC, the NKP does not need to identify itself with either the West European or the Moscow "model," but can seek to establish a national "Norwegian" image. Things could change, however, if Norway were to become a member of the EC or if a new cold war were to break out. In the former case, the NKP would probably have to seek some kind of ideological and political adaptation to the other communist parties in the EC. In the latter case, a return to the situation of the '50s would be likely. The worst possibility for the NKP would be a combination of the above-mentioned alternatives: EC membership *and* new East-West tension. But this would mean a critical situation for Norwegian as well as European politics in general and is a rather hypothetical possibility that will not be discussed here. It goes without saying that the NKP is still strongly opposed to Norwegian membership in the EC. The possibility of the NKP taking part in cooperation between communist (and socialist) parties inside the EC is apparently considered as too remote to receive any attention in the NKP public discussion.

The greatest problem for the NKP is that it is numerically a very small party. Recent polls gave it less than half a percent of the votes. This does not exactly increase its attractiveness as a partner in Norwegian politics. Still the new NKP leadership argues strongly, and perhaps more so than the former one, in favor of unity of the labor movement and of close cooperation between communists, socialists, and social democrats. The "Maoist" AKP is categorically rejected as a possible candidate for cooperation. The NKP admits having some "problems of delimitation towards the AKP"[29] After refusing to join the SV, the NKP is having great difficulties in establishing relations at all to this party. Perhaps for this reason, but perhaps also on the basis of a more fundamental reassessment of international and national political developments, there are signs that the party is reconsidering its attitudes to social democracy:

> Of far greater importance to us than our problems with SV and other independent left groupings, are our problems with social democracy, which had and still has the hegemony in the Norwegian labour movement. A large part of our educational training programme will have to deal with the question of unity (of the labour movement) and the conditions of social democracy.[30]

The Chairman of the NKP, Knutsen, declares it to be a task of primary importance "to see to it that we take neither a sectarian nor an opportunistic attitude to the DNA and the labour movement." He considers sectarianism as "practically a rejection of the social democrats and large sections of organized labour." "Opportunism," on the other hand, is

> the equally shortsighted tendency of closing one's eyes to the absolute necessity of developing a maximum of open, fundamental and constructive criticism of social democracy as an ideology and of DNA in all fields where this party fails and makes errors in practical politics, domestically as well as in foreign policy.[31]

Interestingly enough, he speaks of "the ever increasing possibilities of cooperation" in the struggle for peace, international trade unionism, and "anti-imperialistic solidarity," as well as safeguarding and extension of democratic rights and the struggle to improve the living conditions of the working class.[32]

CONCLUSION

Norwegian foreign policy can only to a very limited extent be explained by reference to ideology, socialist or otherwise. Generally speaking, official postwar foreign policy has been based on a broad consensus between the Labour Party (DNA) on the one hand and the bourgeois parties on the other.

Significant changes in Norway's position on European and Atlantic questions are not very likely to occur in the foreseeable future, and certainly not as a result of ideological developments at party level. The DNA stands for continuity as regards both Atlantic and West European cooperation.

Given DNA's dominant position and the corresponding weakness of the SV and NKP, there is no "socialist" alternative to the clearly reformist, social democratic, western-oriented policy of the DNA government. The relatively strong representation of the SV (including the NKP) in the present Storting has not changed this situation.

The SV and NKP are both revolutionary parties as far as their *goals* are concerned. But they advocate the introduction of socialist reforms by peaceful, democratic *means*. So it is rather difficult to get any clear idea of the revolutionary character of the socialist transformation process that is their objective. For all practical purposes, both seem to have accepted the need to work on the basis of the existing political system and have made it one of their primary tasks to influence the DNA in a more "radical" direction.

In view of the concern that has been voiced about the possible implications of West European socialism for Atlantic relations, one should distinguish carefully between two aspects. The first is its implications for intra-Western relations. There is perhaps still some reason to be skeptical about the "independence" of some West European communist parties. As far as Norway is concerned, however, there is no reason at all to expect a more pro-Soviet attitude—at the expense of relations with the United States—as a result of socialist party attitudes. (In this connection it should be noted that the SV is critical of *both* superpowers.)

On the other hand, if Atlantic relations were to become strained because of what was genuinely *internal* development within Norwegian social democracy, or within democratic socialist parties in some other West European countries (or at the regional West European level), then this would no doubt create the need for a thorough reexamination of the whole basis of what is called the Atlantic community.

NOTES

1. Cf. the Valen Marthinussen analysis published in *Arbeiderbladet*, Nov. 16, 1975.
2. Norges Markedsdata A/S.

3. H. Valen, "National Conflict Structure and Foreign Politics: The Impact of the EEC Issue on Perceived Cleavages in Norwegian Politics," *European Journal of Political Research* 4 (1976), p. 49.

4. Speech at the Socialist Economists' Association, May 10, 1975.

5. Speech given at the AUF Congress, 1975.

6. Ibid.

7. Ibid.

8. SV Prinsipp-Program, 1975, p. 18, ff.

9. Speech at Socialist Economists' Association, May 10, 1975.

10. Ibid.

11. Speech at the Norwegian Student Society, February 22, 1976.

12. *Arbeiderbladet*, January 22, 1976.

13. Interview given to *Dagbladet*, March 12, 1976.

14. Ibid.

15. For an analysis of the situation in the NKP at this crucial stage, see Per Egil Hegge, "'Disunited' Front in Norway," in *Problems of Communism*, May-June 1976, pp. 49–58.

16. H. Valen, op. cit., p. 67.

17. M. G. Knutsen, "Kommunistene foran store oppgaver" (Communists facing great challenges), [article in] *Verden og vi* no. 3/1976, p. 291.

18. M. G. Knutsen, "Veien fram for NKP og venstrekreftene" (The road ahead for the NKP and the left forces), pamphlet issued on the basis of his report to the NKP Congress, Oct. 31–Nov. 2, 1975, p. 15.

19. "Kommunistene foran store oppgaver," p. 291.

20. Prinsipp-Program, p. 12.

21. Ibid.

22. H. I. Kleven, *Var strategi* (Oslo: 1975), p. 113.

23. Ibid., p. 114.

24. "Veien fram . . .," p. 17.

25. *Friheten*, Oslo, no. 26 (1976), p. 9.

26. "Veien fram . . .," p. 16.

27. *Friheten*, no. 26 (1976), p. 9.

28. Ibid.

29. *Vart Arbeid*, no. 4 (1976).

30. Deputy Chairman H. I. Kleven at the NKP Congress, April 1976. *Vart Arbeid*, no. 4 (June 1976), p. 5.

31. "Veien fram . . .," p. 13.

32. Ibid., pp. 13, 19.

CHAPTER

6

THE FRENCH SOCIALIST PARTY AND WESTERN RELATIONS

Jacques Huntzinger

On the occasion of the Congress of Epinay in June 1971, which saw the birth of the Socialist Party and established Mitterand's authority over it, there was a very heated debate about the Socialist Party's affiliation with the Second International. Was the new party to remain formally linked with socially democratic parties that were greatly influenced by the cold war, Atlanticism, anticommunism, and reformism; or, on the contrary, establish a distance in relation to social democracy without, in so doing, joining the Third International, and thus appear as the expression of a "regenerated" socialism in Europe? Under Mitterand's influence, it was decided by a slight majority to remain a member of the Second International.

The Socialist Party adopted its political program at the Suresnes Convention in the spring of 1972. On this occasion, a broad debate was initiated over France's affiliation with the Atlantic Alliance. Should France remain linked to the United States and the Western system through an alliance inherited from the cold war and anti-Sovietism, or, on the contrary, should she set out on a path of European neutrality? There again, by a small majority, the convention rejected the anti-Atlantic amendment.

In January 1976, in connection with the election of the European Parliament by universal suffrage, a new debate began within the Socialist Party on Europe, on the compatibility of the building of socialism with the construction of Europe, on the nature of the European Economic Community. Finally, however, the leadership committee of February 1,

---

This paper was translated by Alice Roper, Department of Foreign Languages, University of New Orleans. The final update was translated by Kathryn Wildgen, also of the Department of Foreign Languages, University of New Orleans.

acting under Mitterand's influence, confirmed the French Socialists' fundamental position in favor of the election of the European Parliament by universal suffrage.

These three examples will illustrate what the foreign policy of the Socialist Party is: it is the image of the party itself, in its diversity, its ambiguities, its contradictions, but also in its originality and dynamism. This fact can be explained by two factors: the origins and the characteristics of the Socialist Party.

THE TRIPLE ORIGINS OF THE SOCIALIST PARTY

Concerning these origins, it is known that the Epinay Congress of June 1971 created the Socialist Party. The aforementioned Congress can be considered like the Bad Godenberg Congress in reverse. It was the congress of unification of French socialist currents, then scattered into divers formations. This unification would be accomplished around François Mitterand. But unity was accompanied by a renewal marked by a return to the sources of French socialism: the priority of ideology over practical politics, the appeal to the double Marxist and Prud'hommian tradition that had always animated French socialism, the affirmation of the full originality of democratic socialism vis-a-vis both communism and reformism, and the will to develop this socialist current in French politics, a strategy of the union of leftist forces expressed notably by the electoral alliance and the establishment of a common program of government with the Communist Party; such were the fundamental points of this return to sources.

But the Socialist Party is not solely the product of the Epinay Congress or the project of renewing the SFIO (Section francaise de l'Internationale ouvriere). G. Defferre, A. Savary, P. Mauroy as well as the CERES (Comite d'Etudes Regionales Economiques et Sociales), regrouping the "young Turks" of the left wing of the SFIO, all played an important role in favor of the socialist revival before 1971. Because of this fact, many leaders of the former SFIO Party, both from the left and moderate wings, will be found in the management bodies of the Socialist Party. Thus they express very diverse feelings in matters of foreign policy, some traditional, others more radical. For example, the former Secretary for International Relations of the SFIO, R. Pontillon, was one of the principal protagonists of the Epinay Congress, as was Jean-Pierre Chevenement. These two men have very different views on international politics and notably on the Atlantic system.

On the other hand, many years have elapsed since Epinay, years marked by one event, the presidential election of 1974. Because of

Mitterand's campaign and its results, the Socialist Party found a new division: the influx of new militants and the entrance of men and groupings heretofore outside the Socialist Party—M. Roccard, E. Pisani, J. Delois, United Socialist Party (PSU) militants, Leftist Christians, the development of the political activity of the party, the widening of its audience in public opinion and in new social strata up to then estranged from socialism. Obviously, however, all these new contributions grafted themselves on a still young and not yet stabilized formation.

At the present, the Socialist Party is thus a combination of several elements: the SFIO, the Epinay Congress, the presidential election of 1974. The fusion has not yet taken place. This triple origin explains the present character of the Socialist Party. The dominant trait is the coexistence of elements that can be either contradictory or complementary.

THE CHARACTERISTICS OF THE SOCIALIST PARTY

First, the Socialist Party is very diverse in its makeup. There coexist at every level of the party orthodox Marxists, Prud'hommian independents, classical social democrats, socialist-leaning technocrats, and pure empiricists.

Whence the development of currents and subcurrents. But the Socialist Party has always united around its first secretary, François Mitterand, completely accepts his authority and decisions, and recognizes him as an arbitrating power in case of an important political controversy. Such was the case, for example, on the occasion of the debate on the European Parliament. The fact that Mitterand has become one of the primary figures in the socialist movement and an international personality has reinforced this process. It can even be stated that the present first secretary benefits from a charismatic authority within the Party which has developed since 1974. Given this fact, the foreign policy of the Socialist Party can just as easily be variable according to the statements of different members or unified if the first secretary decides to give his opinion on a given topic. Thus, diversity of currents and unity around the first secretary constitute the first characteristic of the Socialist Party.

The second is the coexistence of the old and the new. The triple origin of the Party explains the fact that it is the bearer of both the results of the pro-Atlantic and anticommunist cold war, and the era of the Gaullist detente and the opening to the Third World. The old and the new find themselves closely involved in the political options of the Socialist Party, therefore in its foreign policy. The old, that is, the SFIO of 1947, is still very much present, indeed more than one would think, and explains the continued existence of the principal European, Atlantic, and Mid-Eastern options of the party. The new, that is, Epinay and after Epinay, explains the evolution of the defense policy, the policy toward the Third World, the new aspect of the European policy.

The third characteristic of the Party is the dialectic of opposition over more than the last 15 years. This opposition has been continuous, absolute, and almost systematic, all the more so since today it is founded on rather different bases than those that motivated the hostility of the SFIO to De Gaulle in the 1960s. The radicalization of French socialism has led to the establishment of the Party's opposition on more ideological grounds (the struggle against exploitation, the anticapitalist strategy, victory over the conservative forces of the right represented by the present governments). This long period of opposition has removed the Party from dossier and political practice and this has played a role especially in the area of international affairs and defense. Consciously or not, the Socialist Party, although it has a great number of local elected officials and has taken on a strategy of electoral conquest of power through the union with the left, has placed itself in the opposition and has settled there. But recently things have changed; the results of the 1974 presidential election, the sudden success of the Party in the district elections of March 1976, and the indications of the present polls have made it discover the possibility it has of rising rapidly to power. Now at least, leaders and militants have realized the problem posed to the Party in what concerns its capacity for management and the transformation of a given society. What part should be accorded to the principles and options of the program established in 1972 and what part to the political, economic, social, and international realities, the constraints imposed on all governments? Everyone finds that the first objective is henceforth to act in such a way that a socialist government can hold firm. There is the principal new factor arising within the Party since 1975. It has been expressed in several of Mitterand's and of Mauroy's statements, it has inspired the principal considerations of the national secretariat (Chantilly and Blois seminars), it gives life to the present projects of the Party. The evolution of the Party in the area of security and defense policy, the establishment of figures for the cost of economic and social reforms, the consideration of a commercial and economic policy, the balancing of the Mid-East policy, and the careful study of the problems posed by Atlantic relations are some of its elements.

In summary: dialectic of the diversity of the party versus the unity around Mitterand, dialectic of the old and the new, dialectic of opposition and power all characterize the Socialist Party in France.

THE THREE LANGUAGES OF THE FOREIGN POLICY OF THE SOCIALIST PARTY

What we have just stated explains that several languages coexist within the Socialist Party in the domain of international relations.[1] The first language goes back to the essential terms of European social democracy, although it "Frenchifies" them. Taking into account the break between the Western and international systems, it emphasizes the Soviet politico-military threat and the interdependence of the Western system. It does not contest France's affiliation with the Western system, the current relations between France, America, and the European states, the institutions established in the 1950s (the Atlantic Alliance, OECD (Organization for Economic Cooperation and Development), EEC, and the like. It takes into account the dependence of the French economy and commerce in relation to the other European states, and it emphasizes the ideological community of the Western world; but it remains attached to France's freedom of action and to the development of democratic socialism in Europe. From this point of view, R. Pontillon and P. Mauroy can not be confused with Helmut Schmidt.

On the contrary, there exists within the Socialist Party a language of a progressive origin. The most worrisome threat for a socialist France would not be Soviet, but Western in origin. This intervention could take several forms: a change in diplomatic relations, French isolation, speculation in currency, commercial boycott. The Chilean Affair, the statements of Henry Kissinger in the spring of 1976 on the internal evolution of West European societies, and the Italian election have fed these reactions and developed these analyses. A socialist France would have to develop a policy of isolation, of self-defense, made necessary by the fact that the socialist splinter planted in the skin of capitalism would provoke negative reactions. On this score, for example, too great a participation in the EEC system would be dangerous for the development of French socialism. This is to some extent the rhetoric of rupture masked by the thesis of "missionary" socialism. This thesis can be called "gaullic-socialism"; it is very much in keeping with the national temperament. It is found partly in the CERES but also within the present majority of the party (Joxe, Questiaux, Current, theses of the Democratic University Movement).

Then there exists a third language, halfway between social democratic language and the Gaullo-socialist language. To simplify, it could be called the "Mitterandist" language. It seeks to establish an equilibrium between ideology and politics, between the old and the new, and above all it is a dialectical language. Taking into account what the Socialist Party is presently in its diversity, and taking into account both the heritage of the cold war and the results of detente, and taking into account French interests and the objectives of socialism, it constantly vacillates between the social democratic propositions and Gaullo-socialist proposals to make modest strides and to bring about new balances. Mitterand's bearing is then very "Jauresian." It is essential because it is what gives impetus to the whole foreign policy of the Socialist Party. Mitterand had been chosen as first secretary in 1971 because of his prestige and personality, but also because of his position of balance between the different factions of the Party. Very logically, therefore, when he began to intervene actively in the domain of international relations he exercised a decisive role. He was the only one capable of making everyone accept a given position.

Is the Socialist Party neo-Gaullist or Atlanticist? Does it have a double language, progressive for public opinion and the militants, and social democratic for the secretariat? What are its positions in the area of the Common Market construction? What is its position toward the United States? An easy answer to these questions is not possible. We can read the Socialist Party's foreign policy only with the grid furnished by the analysis of its short history and characteristics. It is this grid that provides the key to the present dialectic: the gradual construction of an original foreign policy through the interaction of extremely diverse positions through the influence of the first secretary. Hence, the observer's impression of a sort of "artistic fuzziness."

EUROSOCIALISM

What is it about? The Socialist Party's 1972 platform states the following goal: "A Europe on the march to socialism." This prospect has certainly become the number one objective of the Party in the domain of foreign policy because it appears as the sole means of building a socialist body within the Western system. "The building of Europe in the perspective of socialism appears in our country as the best possibility of resisting imperialism."[2] Failing that, the French socialist experiment would risk wilting in its hostile environment, and in any case it would mean the blocking of the development of socialism in Western Europe. It is a question then of remaining within the Western system while pushing for the development of socialist experiments within it. In order to do this, the best thing is not to export a model, but to develop relations between the European socialist parties, to compare the experiments and strategies of these different parties, to reinforce solidarity with the socialists closest to the French Socialist Party. It is not a question simply of accepting the coexistence of the different socialist parties and different national experiences, above all because, at the present, that leads to assuring the supremacy of traditional social democracy over European socialism. Thus, between the refusal of exportation of a French model and the refusal of simple coexistence of national parties, a strategy is gradually being elaborated: developing a dynamics among the whole of Western socialist parties that permits the strengthening of the chances of building a Western socialism that is both specific and diversified. This is what can be termed Eurosocialism.

The organization of the Paris Conference of Southern European Socialist Parties (January 1976), the Elsinore Talks Among the European Socialist Leaders (January 1976), the action of the Socialist Party within the SPD (German Socialist Party) following the spring 1976 meeting between Mitterand and Willie Brandt are its significant elements. In the same way, the fact that the emblem of the fist and the rose is henceforth the official insignia of the Danish, Dutch, Belgian, Luxembourgian, and Swiss socialist parties is not devoid of meaning.

It seems that in 1975 the Socialist Party first had the idea of building something special among the southern European socialist parties. Mediterranean socialism seemed to correspond to something valid considering the similar problems posed to the different parties: competition and cooperation with the important communist parties, the role of ideology in Mediterranean socialism, the importance given to reforms of the economic structure, cultural similarities. In May 1975 Mitterand took the initiative to invite on an informal basis the principal southern European socialist leaders to Lache (Landes). It was a question of seeing to what extent it was possible to establish links among the Mediterranean socialist parties so as to carry more weight in the socialist movement and to facilitate the development of socialist experiments of another type than that existing in northern Europe. The Portuguese affair was the starting point of this initiative. During the whole crisis of the Portuguese revolution, Mitterand caused the Socialist Party to accept the active support of M. Soares and the Portuguese Socialist Party because he thought that this party was the most capable of opening an original and significant socialist experiment after the legislative elections, in conjunction with the whole of leftist forces (participation of the Socialist Party in the Committee for Solidarity and Friendship with Democracy and Socialism in Portugal created in August 1975 on H. Wilson's initiative). The meeting in Lache paved the way for the Paris Conference on June 25, 26, 1976. This conference brought five parties together: The Belgian Socialist Party, the PSOE (Spanish Socialist Party), the Socialist Party (France), the PSI (Italy), and the PSP (Portugal) plus numerous observers (Socialist International, European Trade Union Confederation, Yugoslavian People's Alliance, the Luxembourgian, Dutch, Finnish, and Swiss Socialist Parties). The theme of reports and discussion was how to make Southern European socialism the lever of the new concepts of European socialism. It must be admitted that the conference did not accomplish all its goals because of the varying degrees of enthusiasm or lack of commitment. (The semi-defection of the PSP in the absence of Soares and the absence of a high-level delegation from the Italian Socialist parties were indications of this lack of commitment.) Certainly the idea of the development of a socialist current that would be distinct from both social democracy and the Western communist current was accepted by everyone.[3] But the Socialist Party admitted that the development of a Eurosocialism could not be accomplished solely among the Mediterranean socialist parties because, in point of fact, there is no real ideological and political split between these parties and the northern socialists. A given Scandinavian or Benelux Party is more open and dynamic than a given Mediterranean Party—the Congress of the Swedish Social Democratic Party, September 1975, or the Doctrinal Congress of the PSB (Benelux Party) attests to that. This fact was brought up by the Socialist Party secretariat at the time of the Blois Seminar in May 1976. This said, there remains the fact that Mitterand is the man who opened the dialogue among the Mediterranean socialist parties. There remains the privileged dialogue among these Mediterranean parties and there remains a common sentiment among these parties that can be called into play in the actions of the socialist movement.

The second aspect of this policy is the Socialist Party's action within the Socialist International. Mitterand was anxious to strengthen the weight of the Socialist Party there in order to limit the domination exercised by traditional social democracy. Elected vice president at the last Congress, he actively participated in all the meetings, notably the meeting of the leaders. At the present time, the primary concern is preparing the next Congress, of 1977, which will be very important. There will be the election of a new president and secretary general. The Socialist Party wishes the election of dynamic personalities open to the whole range of European socialist currents, as well as the adoption of structural reforms (the development of opportunities for reflection on economic and social doctrinal problems, the transfer of headquarters, and so on).

It is a question of revitalizing the socialist international and making it a framework adapted to the development of Eurosocialism in all its parts. The Elsinore talks among the European leaders of the Socialist International (January 18–20, 1970) were very meaningful in this regard: the discussion hit on economic problems (opposition between the partisans of market economy and planned economy) in connection with the Schmidt report on the economic situation and, following Mitterand's report, on relations with the communist parties. This was not a head-to-head

Franco-German discussion but rather a general discussion among all 18 participants. Thus the Dutch, Belgian, and Italian parties, as well as O. Palme, made numerous criticisms of the liberal proposals presented by Schmidt.

The third aspect of Eurosocialism consists of the relations with the SPD (German Socialist Party). A great deal could be said about the history of the relationship between the Socialist Party and the SPD. In fact, the Socialist Party, notably its international secretariat, and Mitterand have always thought that it was very important to succeed in establishing fruitful relations with the SPD; first because the SPD remains the pivot of European social democracy, strongly influencing the European socialist movement, and second because it currently governs the most powerful state in Western Europe, the Federal Republic of Germany. Already, on the eve of the first round of the May 1974 presidential elections, Mitterand had sent several representatives (Pontillon and Roccard) to meet with the ministers of Schmidt's governmnt to discuss monetary problems and to gain information about eventual German support of France's entry in the "snake." But the difficulties between the two parties, which have very different concepts of socialism (one of which is in power and the other in the opposition), are inevitable. Nineteen seventy-five was an even cooler year for relations between the two parties because of the Lache initiative. On the other hand, in spite of appearances, in spite of the "witch hunt" affair in the German government, and despite Schmidt's statements on Italy, 1976 was a productive year. In effect, on the request of the SPD, Mitterand and Schmidt met in Bonn in April 1976. This meeting concluded very positively, even if there was a certain reticence surrounding the results. Three task forces were set up between the two parties (for social projects, North-South relations, and European problems). The first group may have an important role because it will permit an in-depth discussion between the two on the themes of planning, nationalization, self-management, and economic reforms. It must be remembered that the personal relations between Mitterand and Brandt have become very good since their first meeting in February 1974. It is indisputable that the Socialist Party is presently anxious to establish good relations of cooperation and confidence, even if within the Socialist Party feelings toward the SPD are diverse, and perhaps even reversed.

The last aspect of Eurosocialism is the most recent. It refers to the reactions of the Socialist Party to the Kissinger statements on the incompatibility of Western European leftist experiments containing communist participation with the maintenance of the Atlantic system. The Socialist Party reacted, mentioning three things specifically: on the one hand it is the prerogative of each people to choose freely its political future, and leftist governments, including communist elements, are perfectly conceivable. But it is natural that this poses a problem for the United States; in this case it is up to the United States to make a decision. In any event, the Socialist Party will not unilaterally give up the Atlantic Alliance nor question its friendship with the American people.[4] Mitterand had already used this same language at Elsinore: "We will not allow a world strategy which would imply a change in our internal political strategy to be imposed upon us." We can conclude that Mitterand's talks with Kissinger in Washington in November 1975 permitted the first secretary to enunciate these three points.

THE EEC (EUROPEAN ECONOMIC COMMUNITY)

Since Epinay, two dates have been important in determining the Socialist Party's European policy: 1973 with the Bagnolet Convention, and winter 1976 with the European Parliament and Tindemans Report affairs.

The Socialist Party is a European party and in this regard it has continued the tenets of the SFIO. It is favorable to the development of Common Market policies, to the enlargement of the European Economic Community, to Europe as a political entity, to the democratization of institutions, and to the election of the Parliament by universal suffrage. But unlike the SFIO, the Socialist Party is no longer a classical European party. Its origins, its makeup, and its strategy cause the fundamental choice no longer to be Europe for Europe, but "Europe on the march toward socialism." Moreover, everyone in the Socialist Party is European, each in his own way. Some are Europeans out of conviction, by tradition, or by belief in European unity; others think of the advantages of social and economic solidarity for a leftist government; still others pay lip service to the idea because they know it is no longer possible to conceive of France outside the EEC, although they see all the risks therein for the building of socialism. Mitterand has played an important role in pushing the development of a European policy halfway between classical Europeanism and the Gaullo-socialist theses. The Bagnolet Convention sought to deepen the party's positions and to effect a general agreement on the delicate problem of the compatibility of the construction of socialism and the development of the Community. Let's say that the Convention ended in a tie between the committed Europeanists (R. Pontillon, P. Mauroy, and G. Jacquet) and the skeptical or conditional Europeans (CERES, N. Questiaux, P. Joxe). Mitterand developed a balanced position expressed in the final motion:

> The platform of the party and the Grenoble Congress have come out in favor of the building of a Europe on the march toward socialism. This choice is fundamental. The Party must emphatically confirm its European policy, but it must more precisely define the objectives it designates for action in order to hasten the construction of an independent, open, and socialist Europe.

Mitterand used all his influence to gain acceptance of the proposition of the pursuit of European construction without preliminary or delay. The Europe to be built cannot immediately be a socialist Europe. The Socialist Party must choose to participate in its construction while maintaining its fundamental preoccupations. In the final analysis, there were two interpretations of the final motion of Bagnolet: the Europeanists saw it as a formal ratification of their propositions while the skeptical and conditional Europeans saw the rough draft of a concept critical of the EEC and the proposition of conditional participation in the Common Market enterprise. This can be called the Bagnolet misunderstanding. Therefore the debate on Europe was reborn within the Socialist Party at the end of 1976 on the occasion of the European Parliament election affair. N. Questiaux's departure from the secretariat already meant that the first secretary and the national leaders of the Socialist Party were remaining faithful to the classical concept of Europe. This was to be confirmed in the European Parliament affair. Debate on determining the Party's attitude toward election reform was lively. All the European and anti-European sensibilities came out into the open. The partisans of "national independence" collided with the partisans of "Europe." Then after allowing it to develop, Mitterand cut off debate:

> The European Parliament exists. This debate has been resolved ever since the signing of the Treaty of Rome. Such is reality. Therefore, it is not a question today of taking a position for or against the Parliament, but of knowing how it will be elected. At the present time the existence of the European Parliament is nowhere being called into question. Election by universal suffrage will give it the authority and prestige of which it is now deprived and will clearly establish in public opinion the European idea which has up to now been fuzzy. A decision was made in December 1973 at Bagnolet. . . . For a socialist, a large scale political policy must be substituted for the economic power of big capital. . . . Europe will either be socialist or not, and it is now appropriate to pave the way for the massive entry of workers into European institutions and the intellectualization of the struggle.[5]

The first secretary's proposition consists in saying that the problem of the European Parliament election must be separated from all other aspects of the European question (the extension of the powers of the

Parliament, the Tindemans Report, European defense, and so on), and, on the specific point of the election, one must be faithful to one's convictions and positions. This was then a firm "yes" to the election of the European Parliament by universal suffrage. The leadership committee of February 1 finally adopted this proposition; only the CERES voted against it (97–34).

The union of socialist parties of the EEC had decided in November 1974 upon the elaboration of a common program on a European scale that should be worked out by the liaison bureau of the union.[6] The Socialist Party is very actively participating in the elaboration and hopes that it will result in the establishment of a common electoral platform for the European Parliament elections.

Does that mean that traditional Europeanism has again become the law of the Socialist Party? Not at all, as the attitude adopted toward the Tindemans Report has clearly demonstrated. Everyone quickly agreed to reject the Report. Already at Elsinore the socialist parties as a whole had shown themselves to be very reserved regarding the Report. Mitterand had then stated that it did not respond to socialist preoccupations. This position was taken again by the Socialist Party in February 1976:

> It begins from a concept which does not correspond to the economic and social reality of Europe and its propositions are extremely insufficient insofar as the institutional aspect takes an exaggerated precedence over the very substance of the union and on the will of a Europe which today is very far from existing. In reality, this Report corresponds both to the political position of the man who wrote it and to the present state of Europe. On the whole, the Tindemans Report expresses a favorable attitude toward the Europe which has failed and admits that it is in no position to propose another.

This is a rejection of the Tindemans Report in the name of socialism. It has nothing to do with classical Europeanism. Thus one can assert that the present Europeanism of the Socialist Party is completely different and can only be understood in the light of Epinay. Mitterand recently gave an important speech on Europe at the Seminar of the European Left concerning the Tindemans Report (May 1976). There he very clearly explained what the Europeanism of the Socialist Party is:

> Europe is, first, the Common Market. We must begin with what we have at our disposal. This Europe is a part of our heritage. Even if it is contestable, American, capitalist, full of red tape, annoying, devoid of meaning, we must take it as it is and try to initiate from this point a different approach without making a *tabula rasa*. The Common Agricultural Policy has failed because of world capitalism which has

> passed into another phase of its expansion. It has failed because of the absence of a common monetary policy. It has failed because of De Gaulle. The danger today is of an American or Atlantic Europe. The time for true Europeans is ripe. Notably West Germany now considers Europe as a means and not as an end. Only Socialism is capable of returning elan, vitality, and creativity to Europe.

ATLANTIC RELATIONS

> France belongs to the western world, to the Atlantic world. It is a participant in an alliance, an Atlantic Alliance. And the problem for France is to determine whether it is good to separate itself from this security system. When I answer this question I'll say yes, on condition that we have another system.[7]

The Socialist Party does not favor the departure of France from the Western system, but it is a question of defining a socialist appproach to it, even though the Western world with which it is related is not socialist. Two problems are posed: 1) the attitude toward the Western socio-economic system; and 2) the attitude toward the Western military system.

The Socialist Party seeks a balance between confrontation and participation. The basic option seems to be "the critical presence"—presence and critical action in the international financial, economic, and monetary institutions. For the Socialist Party the Western economic system appears more and more as the privileged sphere of American economic power, hence the acceptance of the proposition of American economic imperialism, even if debate exists as to the political utility of such a statement. But the Socialist Party considers the manifestations of this American economic power indubitable; the take-over of the world energy market, the recuperation of the Mid-East, the limitation of the development of the EEC by the Nixon Round, the creation of an agri-power capable of being used particularly against the Third World, and the characteristic actions of the American multinational companies. The Socialist Party's attitude toward the Nixon Round, the Kingston agreements, the world economic crisis, and the North-South Conference are explained by this analysis. In this domain, the consensus is real within the Socialist Party. Nevertheless, some consider it important to denounce vigorously American power and the threat to the freedom of peoples and the Western socialist experiment posed by American imperialism and the multinational companies. Others, thinking of the security of Europe, the balance of forces, and the Atlantic Alliance, consider that they must be more moderate in form because it is necessary to handle Franco-

American friendship very carefully. From this standpoint, Atlantic sentiment is very diverse inside the Party.

As for the security of the Atlantic Alliance, the debate has always existed in the Party. But it has evolved. First, there was the debate on principles at the Suresnes Convention of 1972 to ascertain whether a socialist France should remain in the Alliance. The Socialist Party decided in favor of maintaining the Alliance but without the restoration of the NATO organizations abandoned in 1966. Since then, this position has remained unchanged, and up to now no one has proposed a formal revision of this attitude.

RECENT CHANGES IN FRENCH-AMERICAN RELATIONS

Two important changes occurred in early 1977: the change in administration in the United States with the arrival of Jimmy Carter and a new team at the White House; and the success of the French Left in the municipal elections of March 1977 and the weakening of the authority and the influence of President Giscard d'Estaing. These two changes went in the same direction as far as the relations between the PS and the West are concerned.

Without having yet defined in a precise fashion a new policy regarding Eurocommunism and the Left in Europe, President Carter has made a certain number of gestures that seem destined to facilitate the establishment of normal relations between a government of the United Left in Paris and the United States. The April 7th declaration of the State Department, the open attitude of most of the young people responsible for the European questions posed by Cyrus Vance, the departure of Mr. Loewenstein are the principal aspects of this rapprochement. Washington seems inclined to demonstrate more pragmatism regarding European changes than during the tenure of Mr. Kissinger, even if the Democratic administration maintains great precautions and a certain uneasiness in the face of the rise to power of various communist parties.

In a parallel fashion, electoral victories of the French Left have forced the Democratic administration to accept these new responsibilities. And certain results have followed in the area of transatlantic relations. One can consider that the "Mitterandist" approach is winning out over other conceptions. It is a question today of reconciling the firmness of ideological commitments with harsh reality. And, notably, it is a question of maintaining a cordial relationship with the U.S. government, with the European capitals, with the European Commission, even if it is not a question of reintegrating NATO, nor of entering Eurogroupe, nor of accepting the monetary agreements of Kingston, or the reform of the IMF. It is a question of maintaining good relationships with the great Western powers and of preserving a climate of confidence despite the difficulties arising through communist participation in government, the nationalizations, and the application of the common program.

The private meetings of Messrs. Cot and Roccard, the national leaders of the PS, with Cyrus Vance in January 1977, the trip to Washington of Robert Pontillon, international secretary of the PS, in May 1977, and the trip of François Mitterand to the United States in the fall of 1977, show that the changes that have occurred on both sides of the Atlantic, if they have not altered the essence of things, have at least permitted a modification of the climate of cooperation.

The United States and French socialism seem to understand each other better today, even if they do not fully accept each other.

NOTES

1. J. Huntzinger, "La Politique etrangere du P.S.," *Pol. Etrangere*, no. 2 (1975).
2. Final motion of the June 1972 Grenoble Congress.
3. "We are socialism in its reality, in its three dimensions: Political, economic and social." Keynote address by Mitterand, January 24, 1976.
4. Mitterand's statement, RTL, March 3, 1976.
5. *L'Unité*, January 1976.
6. Leadership Conference of the Socialist Parties of the EEC, The Hague, November 1, 1974.
7. Press conference, April 12, 1974.

CHAPTER

7

SOCIALIST PARTIES AND ITALIAN FOREIGN POLICY: REBUILDING A NEW POLITICAL BASE?

Fulvio Attina

A study of political parties and foreign policy can be approached on five levels: that of party ideology and the interpretation of international events; the choices made on questions involving the action or the international position of the country; that of the internal processes of formulating official statements; that of the relation between party programs and ideas in international and foreign affairs and the opinions of the social and economic forces of the country; and that of the party's formal and informal connections abroad. These are complementary and equally useful levels of approach, but the analyses of the foreign policy of European parties that refer to these levels are not great in number; with regard to Italian parties their number is even scantier. These analyses are often either brief essays or related to the political moment. The examination that this study makes of the ideas, programs, and positions taken by the Italian Socialist Party (PSI) and by the Italian Social Democratic Party (PSDI) during the republic experience from 1948 to the present is primarily based on the first two of the above-mentioned levels of approach, because it aims to analyze, above all, the participation of the two parties in the process of formulating a national foreign policy. In fact, during the span of the 30 years examined, first the PSDI (1948–59), and then both parties, gravitated around the government area (except for a few interruptions). For almost three years (October 1966 to July 1969), the parties were joined in the PSU (United Socialist Party) and they shared the same foreign policy program lines. The process of getting the foreign policy concepts of the two parties closer together, uniting, and subsequently parting, thus merits special attention.

THE NEUTRALIST "CONVICTION" (1947–48)

During the first few years following the end of World War II, public opinion and the majority of Italian political forces did not have very clear ideas on the international position of the new republic. During the first governments presided over by De Gasperi, the PSIUP (Italian Socialist Party of Proletarian Unity, the only socialist party of the times) was a firm supporter of the neutralist line that was later also maintained by the two parties resulting from the split of the 25th Congress (January 1947). As early as March 1946, Churchill had warned from Fulton that Europe was already divided in two. But the events of the second half of 1947 (the offer of help for reconstruction by Secretary of State Marshall to all European countries, and the Soviet refusal a few weeks later; the official participation of Italy at the Paris conference on the Marshall Plan; the anti-American declaration at the recently constituted Cominform), placed the two socialist components—PSI and PSLI—before a first reexamination of the neutralist line. The debate lasted almost a year and when Parliament discussed and ratified the European Recovery Program (ERP) accords in July 1948, the convention of the OEEC (Organization for European Economic Cooperation) and the Italo-American agreement, the two parties found themselves in different positions. For Italy, as for other European countries, strong economic assistance would have guaranteed a recovery, and this conviction was shared by public opinion.[1] The Social Democrats (the party was then called the PSLI) adhered to a strictly economic interpretation of the Marshall Plan and voted in favor of ratification, with no intention, however, of abandoning the neutralist line. The PSI, which was out of government, voted against ratification of the accords, because they would have made Italy dependent on the United States.

The basis of this discrepancy was, in fact, a different conception of the common neutralist line. This, in turn, was related to a different perception of the international order and of the possible strategies of its participants. The construction of a socialist Europe was the patrimony of both parties' ideology, but they had deeply divergent attitudes toward the Soviet Union. These ideological considerations were accompanied by different perceptions of the two parties' leaders concerning the configuration of the international system. For the Social Democrats the division of the international system into two blocs was not a rigid and absolute structure. They maintained that within this division the autonomy of Europe was possible by following a line of equidistance from the Soviet Union and the

United States. Within the party this concept was strongly defended by Mondolfo, for whom neutralism could assure peace and the autonomy of Europe because it reinforced the equilibrium of the system. Since neither the OEEC nor the program of American aid required a formal rejection of European equidistance, the vote for ratification did not violate the neutralist line. This was true, however, only if the interpretation of the international order given by the party leaders was also true.[2]

The PSI had, instead, an interpretation quite different from considerations of equilibrium and equidistance. The goal of a socialist Europe and the appeal of the Soviet Union as the land of socialism was related to a perception of the international order as one in which the relations between the two great powers and the other states became more and more exclusive and polarized.[3] In the formation of this perception of the international order, considerations of power had less importance than political-ideological evaluations; the perception of the international order was dictated mainly by the identification of the comparison between the United States and the Soviet Union with that of capitalism and socialism. The vote against ratification of the ERP accords was, thus, an opposition to the forces of international capitalism that intended to relate to internal capitalism. Beneath this perception shared by the entire party, emerged divergencies between the "left" (Nenni, Morandi) and the "center" (Lombardi, Jacometti). For the "left," Europe was the theater of a struggle between American capitalism and Soviet socialism; opposition to American assistance had to be absolute; neutralism and pro-Sovietism were thus confused with international class solidarity. For the "center," the clash between capitalism and socialism did not necessarily correspond to the clash between alignments of states; the opposition to the European Recovery Program could have been conducted on a technical basis that would have protected requirements of autonomy and economic development. Thus neutralism was made concrete in the autonomy of each socialist party's foreign policy.

Jacometti and Lombardi's line was the official party line during the short period (June 1948 to May 1949) when the "Socialist Recovery" had a relative majority in the party. In *Avanti*, Lombardi was able to maintain that the national transformation towards socialism would be insured by a disarmed neutrality, while the rest of the party was convinced that the internal struggle could not take place outside the international struggle since both were concerned with the same class struggle. For Nenni and the "left," the bipolarity of power and the political-ideological heterogeneous nature of the international order greatly limited neutralism and made it almost impossible.

ATLANTICISM AND ANTI-ATLANTICISM (1949–55)

July 1948 saw the ratification of the ERP accords, July 1949 the ratification of the Atlantic Pact; another year of transformations for Europe and of choices for Italy. The Western states (France, Great Britain, Belgium, Holland, and Luxembourg) that had created the European Union (with the Brussels Pact of March 1948) began negotiations, together with the United States and Canada, to constitute an Atlantic Alliance; at the same time the Council of Europe was also taking shape. Meanwhile, the Eastern states were closing their ranks; Yugoslavia was expelled from the Cominform (June 1948); and the Council for Mutual Economic Assistance (COMECON) was born (January 1949). Those who had foreseen a process of increasing polarization on the international scene were proved correct by these events. The Western inclinations of Italian governmental circles would not wait too long to change into Atlanticism under joint pressures from abroad, especially from the United States, and from internal pressures. In fact, the overlapping of international and internal polarization led, in a determining way, to the Atlantic decision. Those who accepted the status quo and those who called for deep changes also referred to external models and to different international relationships. The debate in the two socialist parties was heated and in particular concerned the neutralist line.

Neutralism was widely diffused among the Social Democrats. Thus, the decision to vote in favor of ratification of the pact led to the abstention of a good eleven PSLI delegates, among them Mondolfo and Zagari. It was Saragat who decided the choice of the party. He had already come close to the European Federalist movement and did not believe in neutralism because it would have ended by cutting Italy off from "European civilization"; for this reason he did not hesitate even in the face of splits with other socialists who were also anticommunists but neutralists. The Atlantic choice was imposed upon the Romita socialists at the moment of fusion between the PSLI and SU and the birth of the PSDI (March 1951).[4]

The Atlanticism of the PSDI in the 1950s always favored any initiative to help reinforce the Western bloc against the Eastern bloc; the distinction between the two blocs was, in fact, a distinction between different cultures and civilizations, between different regimes and political patterns. The PSDI, thus, supported every initiative imposed by the logic of the cold war (the cost of rearmament in 1951) and every European-oriented initiative (the Federal Union Pact in 1951, ECSC, EDC, and later the WEU, etc.).

In those years the PSDI was (and would remain so until 1956) the only Italian socialist party represented in the Socialist International. It also shared with other Northern European social democratic parties an opposition to communism. Before the Socialist International (which was quite interested in the matter), the PSDI took a position in favor of the Free Territory of Trieste, protecting the rights of ethnic minorities. The PSDI accepted the Allied decision of October 1954. However, it reaffirmed the principle of the plebiscite, since they, as other Italian parties in those years, were sensitive to a certain nationalism diffused throughout Italian society.

In March 1949 the PSI, on the other hand, had left the COMISCO (Committee of the International Socialist Conferences) due to an absolute disagreement over relations with communist parties by Eastern European communist parties and was against the unity action pact between the PCI and the PSI. These events were part of the debate over Italy's adherence to the Atlantic Pact and they clarified the position assumed by the PSI over the unity of the anti-Atlantic choice as the only choice related to internal and international alignments. The abandonment of neutralism was brought into the party by the Nenni majority which, in view of the split in anti-Fascist unity, was concerned about lining up the Italian working class with the positions of other socialist parties. Thus, not even the PSI escaped the manichean framework of the cold war.

During the entire first legislature, the anti-Atlanticism of the PSI was also pro-Soviet. The government policy toward the Soviet Union was constantly criticized; in 1952 Nenni even went so far as to propose a non-aggression pact with the Soviet Union.

Among the reasons for opposing the Atlantic Pact set forth by Nenni during parliamentary debates on the signing and ratification, some refer to certain national reasons which would have had a stronger appeal after the events of Hungary. The defense of independence and national sovereignty could certainly not have been colored with nationalistic tones typical of the right and was limited to accusations launched at the government for sacrificing national interests to those of the capitalist bloc. In the campaigns against the ECSC, EDC, and WEU, the national motives were confused and suffocated by anticapitalist motives, and these were identified with pro-Sovietism. In the Trieste question, however, the national themes were predominant. All things considered anti-Titoism—which was soon to be abandoned—played a minor role. The PSI supported the legitimacy of the Italian claims on the two zones, accepted the proposal of a plebiscite, and considered as treason the West's memorandum of 1953.[5]

The PSI, which until the mid-1950s was not much different in foreign policy from the PCI, was alert to some changes taking place. The internal picture (consolidation of centrist governments, the split in the labor movement) called for reconsiderations and the international picture took on a new look. The first Soviet thermonuclear bomb (August 1953) seemed to have more of a stabilizing than a destabilizing effect, while the Western will to find a solution to the German problem led to a quick conclusion (within a month) of the constitutive conference of the Western European Union (October 1954). Together with the PCI, the PSI voted against parliamentary ratification of the WEU, but the opposition was not obstructionist as had been threatened. On that occasion, the Chamber approved the Montini order of the day that, in response to the Soviet proposal of November 13, 1954, calling for a pan-European security conference, obliged Italy to become the advocate of a conference for simultaneous arms reductions in Europe. These were some signs of strengthening the European system; of a thaw in the cold war; of erosion on the internal and international fronts; signs which the PSI did not fail to evaluate concretely. Some socialists even took the initiative to distinguish between internal evolution and that on the international level. In the debate on the vote of confidence for the Segni government (July 1955), Nenni proposed collaboration between the democratic parties and the forces of the left, stating "it is possible to differ on the means and methods of our foreign policy without creating insurmountable incompatibilities." The debate on the transfer of American troops from Austria to Italy in that same year was one of the last parliamentary debates in which the PSI agitated strongly in favor of its anti-Atlantic themes. During the 1956 Suez affair, however, the attacks on the Western colonial powers hit the foreign policy of the Italian government only indirectly and marginally. The PSI accepted the government's distinction between "nationalization and freedom of navigation" of the Canal.

The considerations of international security were not alien to moderating the tones of the conflicting positions between the blocs. The PSI was very active in frequently proposing initiatives in favor of disarmament. Between 1955 and 1957, progress on the part of the two superpowers in the field of long-range bombers, the increase of nuclear experiments (28 in 1956 and 48 in 1957), the affirmation of the strategy of massive retaliation, were accompanied by a series of international proposals (the Franco-British plan, the Malik plan, the Rapacki plan, and others) for arms control and disarmament in Europe. The PSI was willing to defend these initiatives in keeping with the pacifist component of its ideology,[6] and was even more so after the Hungarian events when, with the condemnation of Soviet repression, the PSI decreed the end of anti-Atlanticism, considered as pro-Sovietism, and a return, for a short period, to the times of neutralism.[7]

THE EEC (1956–57)

The "return" of the PSI also in the internal political system (the meeting between Praliognan, Nenni, and Saragat, and the end of the unity action pact with the PCI took place in 1956) must be taken into consideration to evaluate the flexible opposition to the Community pacts.[8] The European experience was, and would remain for years, alien to the PSI. Anti-Atlanticism had been extended to any Western initiative in Europe and also, in this way, the PSI had taken its distance from the socialist area of Western Europe. On the other hand, the maturing of a European market could not go unrecognized and, in fact, the first interest of the PSI for European integration had a "technical" character. Very few spoke of Europe as an "autonomous element of world policy in the service of peace," as Nenni expressed it at the 32nd Congress of the party; the majority evaluated the possible beneficial effects of the European Common Market on the Italian productive apparatus and asked that the party become involved in the defense of workers' interests even on a European level, because at this level the industrialists would have organized themselves with agreements and cartels; the government was also asked to maintain control over the economic union.

The European debate within the PSDI was quite different. The party saw in the initiatives of European unification not only a reinforcement of society and Western culture, but also a sign that these initiatives would prevail. In addition, the party saw how correct had been the efforts of their leader, who had been engaged in the European enterprise since the end of the war. Saragat had pursued this goal because he was convinced that the ties with European democracies would have guaranteed the development of Italy.

DETENTE AND ITALY'S INTERNATIONAL POSITION (1958–61)

At the end of the 1950s, Italy became one of the 10 major exporting countries in the world, even though its goods were sent primarily to Euro-Atlantic markets. Imports also increased, but manufactured products coming from industrialized countries increased, as a percentage of the total, more than those of raw materials. Thus, in this way, Italy found itself more closely anchored to the Euro-Atlantic area than it had been after the war. This aspect of Italy's international position was well recognized by the Italian socialists between 1958 and 1962. If the 1958 PSI program was limited to a wish for "a new foreign policy direction rejecting Atlantic over-involvement," a few days before the elections, Nenni had also referred to a nonmilitary dimension of NATO favorable to economic collaboration and to reciprocal aid.[9] The defense of the interests of the workers' movement could not be wedded to a frontal assault any more, but instead required an early agreement on disarmament and security in Europe. The PSI had always been favorable to such proposals and also promoted them in Parliament.[10] The nuclear moratorium from 1958 to 1961 was, in fact, accompanied by an escalation in the missile field. In December 1957, NATO decided to equip itself with nuclear warheads and medium-range missiles (IRBM); in the following March came the agreement (the contents of which were secret) between the United States and Italy for supplying IRBMs with nuclear warheads to NATO bases in Italy. In 1960 and 1961 other agreements of a military nature between the United States and Italy followed. The PSI asked that the contents of the accords on missiles be made public; a motion in this sense was discussed in the Senate in mid-April. The Socialists, who were almost to the point of recognizing the defensive nature and geographic limits of NATO, maintained that the agreement could not be part of the Atlantic Pact and asked the government to take concrete steps towards detente and the elimination of blocs in Europe.

This request was inscribed in the renewed neutralism of the party, which had been obfuscated by the pro-Sovietism of the early 1950s.[11] Neutralism is an essential part of the ideological patrimony of the party and reappears whenever it is not set aside because of other ideological considerations or evaluations of "realpolitik." In fact, the neutralist hypotheses of the late 1950s were tempered by an awareness of the blocs' rigidity and by the necessity of not hindering the process of realignment of the internal picture toward a center-left collaboration.

Meanwhile, on the international front, the Afro-Asian states were achieving independence. The PSI (some sector of the party had valued the neo-Atlantic aspects of certain Christian Democratic sectors as an opening to the emerging countries and not only in the Mediterranean area) proposed that Italy dissociate itself concretely from the imperialistic policies of the other Western countries. Inspired by the neutralist idea, this proposal of somehow relating Italy to the bloc of nonaligned countries that was meeting for the first time in Belgrade in September 1961 was an attempt to give to neutralism a concrete foundation of dialectic and corrosive opposition to the East-West confrontation that was dangerously exhausting detente. In this sense the failure of the Big Four summit in Paris in 1960 was strongly condemned by the Socialists.

The PSDI, on its side, was much less willing to emphasize the relaxation of tension of the cold war in Europe. Saragat's insistence to neutralize and then to deatomize central Europe was considered more imposed by necessity than by conviction.[12] It was true that the Social Democratic party proceeded with extreme caution in European affairs and Atlantic policy. The neo-Atlantic hypothesis had been accepted by some Social Democrats only as a step towards potential relations in the Mediterranean area; on the other hand, the PSDI in 1956 (and also in the future) was pro-Israel in the Middle East war. The Social Democrats had been generous toward the newly independent countries in statements of support for their expectations of equality and development. The ideal of international justice was part of the party patrimony, as well as considerations of international security and equilibrium, on the basis of which the PSDI hoped for an appropriate policy of assistance from the industrial countries to the underdeveloped nations.

Detente in Europe, instead, appeared to the PSDI as a slow process not without difficulties (the Berlin crises in 1958 and 1961) that made unfeasible a relaxation of the Atlantic trust. The cohesion of the Western bloc was not to be questioned (the condemnation of the "force de frappe" of France) and within this bloc American leadership had to be accepted as a guarantee of security (including acceptance of the multilateral nuclear force under conditions determined by Washington). In addition, for the PSDI, the opening of negotiations for the entrance of Great Britain to the EEC (November 1961) and the movement towards the second-phase realization of the EEC treaties (January 1962), constituted further progress for the Western world. Thus the proposal launched by Kennedy in his Philadelphia speech (July 1962), on an Atlantic partnership between Europe and the United States, was received enthusiastically by Saragat, who referred to it several times in the succeeding years.

ACCEPTANCE OF NATO (1961–62)

Meanwhile, the autonomists and part of the left wing of the PSI were deeply involved in a debate on neutralism and on relations with the Third World.[13] This debate was dividing the PSI on matters of internal policy and led to a schism. Basso and Vecchietti considered erroneous the interpretation that Nenni gave to the international scene.[14] Their analysis detected a rising crisis of capitalism in the Third World with which the European socialists had to deal (under the guidance of the Soviet Union, the principal force of socialism). Nenni's interpretation, instead, was suggested by the secondary role the PSI was forced to play during the years of the cold war; for having placed international considerations above internal ones; and for having also, in this manner, placed obstacles in the way of certain national developments. Detente was taking place between Khrushchev's Russia and Kennedy's America; it did not modify the international makeup and did not free anyone from the ties of alliances and from bloc alignments, but precisely for this reason detente permitted the PSI to enter the government. At the 34th Congress of the party, the majority officially stated that the Atlantic Alliance had contributed to peaceful relations in Europe and that it did not contrast with detente. The definitive acceptance of Italy's belonging to NATO took place in January 1962—a strictly defensive and rigidly limited alliance, that, if deserted, would create a fatally dangerous destabilization of peace and the balance of power in the world. Whether or not it was Moro who desired an open acceptance of NATO in order to favor the center-left,[15] it is certain that there prevailed within the PSI the view of international equilibrium as a result of bipolar condominium in the world.[16] During the following years, the relaxation of the nonalignment endeavor and the relationship between the United States and the Soviet Union, with its evolution from the Cuban crisis to the Glassboro meeting (June 1967) left everyone convinced that the choice had been correct. These developments even led to indulgent interpretations of the various roles played by the parties involved in the Vietnam war, at least during the first period of the conflict.

THE FIRST PERIOD OF THE CENTER-LEFT: EUROPEAN CHOICES, EQUILIBRIUM, AND ANTI-DE GAULLISM (1963–66)

On the Vietnam issue the PSDI sided with America. The affinity with the United States constantly inspired Saragat's action at the Foreign Ministry in 1964. Tanassi, his successor as party secretary, maintained that the United States, in defending Vietnam, was defending the freedom of everyone. On the other hand, De Martino, at the 36th PSI Congress (November 1965), while condemning the intervention, acknowledged that the United States could not withdraw if North Vietnam did not agree to begin negotiations. The differences that existed between the two parties did not emerge to the point of disturbing collaboration within the government; nor had this cooperation been disturbed, at the beginning, even by the last debates on the Atlantic multilateral force, when the PSDI was uniformly favorable to the proposal while the PSI was perplexed and divided; not even by the debate on the recognition of the People's Republic of China and its admission to the United Nations, with the PSDI reluctant about any Italian initiative autonomous from the United States, and the PSI completely in favor, as it had been in the past. With the beginning of the center-left, Italy's foreign policy appeared to be a departure from the socialists' interests. For Italy, in reality, the choices and decisions to make in the '60s were politically less important than those taken during the preceding 15 years, but some were indeed anything but secondary in nature.

The inflationary crisis of 1962–63 and the highly negative balance of trade in 1963, which provoked a crisis in the balance of payments for example, were also instrumental in stimulating political initiatives to strengthen Italian exports once again. One aspect of these initiatives was the Socialist parties' contributions to the so-called "Eastern policy" of the center-left, which brought about several visits and agreements with the East European countries (between 1963 and 1965). In this way, while in 1960 exports to the socialist countries were only 2.3 percent of all Italian exports, in 1968, thanks to the agreements with East European countries, these exports had doubled, reaching 5.4 percent. To understand the foreign policy of the socialists in the government, after the so-called "economic miracle" recession was beginning, one must take into consideration the concerns over an international economic system that was showing signs of sluggishness, especially in methods of payments (from the creation of the gold pool and the "Group of Ten" in 1961 and 1962, until the French denunciation of the gold exchange standard and the International Monetary Fund decision to institute Special Drawing Rights in 1965 and 1967). Thus the consideration that the bipolar system had by that time settled at the center (Yugoslavia was partially admitted to COMECON in September 1964), relegating tension to the periphery (the landing of Marines in South Vietnam in March 1965). In addition to considerations of an economic nature, those reasons were the source of the anti-De Gaulle attitude that united the PSI and the PSDI. At that point the two parties were showing an identity of views both in European and Atlantic policies as far as relations among European partners were concerned. They favored the stability of a framework that had to be maintained in order not to upset certain situations contributing to the intensification of commercial exchanges throughout the continent.

The parties had already agreed in 1963 to condemn the French decision to refuse admission of Great Britain to the EEC. By then the PSI had completely accepted the communitarian bonds in their more unitarian forms: reinforcement of the executive expansion of members, direct elections to Parliament. The PSI statements did not differ at all from those of its socialist partner in the government coalition. However, these statements, as clearly appeared in the plan of political unification presented by Saragat at the end of 1964, quite soon proved to be insufficient in the phase of realization, because the two parties still lacked experience at the level of contacts between the government and the Community organs; because their elaboration had been insufficiently discussed and prepared; and because the two parties had not made the necessary contacts with other European socialist parties. These contacts would be delayed even in the years ahead. De Gaulle's opposition to the extension of powers of the Commission took the Italian socialists again by surprise; they found themselves unprepared precisely in an area where increased involvement on the part of the Italian government was necessary. Anti-de Gaullism further consolidated the agreement between the PSI and the PSDI in the months preceding the unification of the two parties. The reproach of the French desertion of the NATO military structures was inspired, in the statements of the two parties, mainly by concerns of strategic balance and the security of detente. The Socialists also felt that Gaullist nationalism hindered the possibilities of cooperation and collective development of the European states that they thought would be achieved within the framework of stability provided by the Alliance.

UNIFICATION: PERSISTENCE AND GRADUALISM OF DETENTE, EROSION OF THE BLOCS (1967–69)

The principal debates during the period of unification (the Mid-East after the Six-Day War, the renewal of the Atlantic Alliance, the signing of the nonproliferation pact) animated the internal dialectic of the Unified Socialist Party and the relations with Christian Democracy along lines of a challenge that was not always clear and not always agreed to by the entire party. The confusion of opinions was immediately reflected in the very same Unification Charter, which, as far as international policy was concerned, was limited to bringing together those ideal principles and concrete objectives maintained or acquired by the two parties during the previous 20 years of political struggle.

During the 1967 Mid-East crisis the PSU refused to permit Italy to be tempted to take any individual action. The various party components were pro-Israel or critical towards Arab expansionism. A policy of "equidistance" of "Mediterranean involvement," as was proposed by Foreign Minister Fanfani, was considered to be an "absurd third force de Gaulle-like position." Pressures were brought to bear on President of the Council Moro, in order to make Italy favor an intervention by the United Nations and the EEC, and these pressures were successful. The Italian Socialists' trust in international organizations is a constant element of their opinion on international policy matters. A United Nations intervention in Vietnam was also advocated on several occasions as was advocated for the Congo. It seems certain, however, that such trust had often overestimated the real capabilities of the United Nations to intervene effectively in certain international crises. In any event, with regard to the Mid-East crisis, one might doubt how deeply thought out were the real issues involved, while the principles of Atlantic loyalty appeared to be totally assimilated.

The debate on the renewal of the Alliance was prudently kept at a low level. The theme of an equal partnership between Europe and the United States was constantly reproposed and had an appealing dimension, even though in reality such a partnership never developed. On the eve of the 20th anniversary of the Pact, the Atlantic Council launched the "Reykjavik signal," or first proposal of a reciprocal and balanced reduction of forces in Europe (May 1968), while two years earlier the Warsaw Pact countries had proposed for the first time a conference on European security. The certainty of detente cautioned against disturbing its gradualism; Nenni, as foreign minister from December 1968 to July 1969, was now convinced that the road to follow was the one of strengthening political cohesion among the West European states. He presented the WEU Council (February 6–7, 1969) with a project drafted by Italian experts on behalf of the organization, concerning the institutionalization of political cooperation. In an Atlantic forum (the Atlantic Council of Washington, April 1969), he renewed the proposal for a pan-European conference that had also been relaunched by the Warsaw Pact countries in Budapest a few months earlier. Nenni proposecd a series of meetings of all European states, including the United States and the USSR, but the Americans dropped the proposal because they preferred to deal directly only with Moscow. In reality, Nenni's moderated and dynamic Atlanticism coexisted in the party with other forms of Atlanticism, such as Lombardi's position, which maintained the impropriety of Italy's presence in an Alliance that did not take concrete initiatives against totalitarian regimes such as the Greek and Portuguese.

Nenni's trust in detente and his will to contribute, were also determining factors in the decision to sign the nuclear nonproliferation treaty. There were a number of subjects; in addition to the technical arguments over controls, the political theme of nuclear condominium of the Big Two and the subordination of the nonnuclear countries was a subject of great interest to the party and led to the request for guarantees that could not be accepted by the Great Powers very easily. Thus Nenni felt that the reservations set forth by the ministers before him and agreed upon by the other Euratom nations were sufficient. The invasion of Czechoslovakia was too serious a matter for detente. Nenni's signing of the nuclear nonproliferation pact on January 28, 1969, was supposed to represent, according to the Socialist leader, the real meaning in favor of a continuing process of detente in Europe.

However, contributing to detente did not mean the Socialists would give up trying to influence the decisions of the Great Powers. In this respect, Foreign Minister Nenni's initiative in officially declaring on January 24, 1969, the Italian intent to diplomatically recognize the

People's Republic of China, even though appropriate and preparatory steps had not yet been taken, assumed a great importance. The Socialists and other leftist parties had always criticized the government for not having wanted to confront and resolve by recognition the subject of relations with communist China. In the early '50s while the Korean war was still going on, the Socialists had posed the problem of recognizing the People's Republic of China. At that time these petitions were a part of the themes of antiimperialist campaigns and international solidarity. Instead, Nenni's initiative in 1969 followed upon the break between China and the Soviet Union, and after the talks concerning the admission of China into the United Nations that had been going on since 1965. France had recognized the People's Republic of China, and Italy itself had opened a commercial office in Peking. Although it was not a question of "if" but "when" to recognize China, America's aversion to direct openings toward China by its allies was very well known. Thus, Nenni's initiative not only tried to place the socialist seal on recognition (which would become definite only two years later) but also had a decisive intent to destabilize bipolarism and to erode the leadership of the two great powers. In fact, neither the United States nor the Soviet Union accepted the international legitimacy of China's role.

THE CRISIS OF THE CENTER-LEFT: OLD DISCREPANCIES AND NEW PROBLEMS (1970–73)

After the schism both the Social Democrats and the Socialists continued to share European involvement of Italy and indeed they asked the government to carry out on a communitarian level global initiatives that would have a strong qualitative impact on the Community. But, at the same time, especially in the PSI, critical opinions were strengthened concerning the procedures whereby the appropriate ministries treated European affairs. In March 1971 the Socialist Scalfari, in a parliamentary interpolation, expressed concern because the government (in the person of its representative on the Community's Council of Ministers) had approved the Werner Report on Economic and Monetary Union, thus involving the country in a matter of maximum importance without previously informing the Parliament. During the debate on the Andreotti government (July 4, 1972), the Social Democrat Orlandi reproposed the institution of a department for the coordination of Community activities. However, despite the demands articulated by the two parties' leaders, no positive response was forthcoming. Furthermore, in a study in the early '70s, the complex Community problems did not receive the necessary attention they merited, particularly following the enlargement of the Community. After the schism, however, the two parties continued to show an equally favorable attitude toward the EEC (somewhat more critical in the PSI than in the PSDI).

Meanwhile, the international scene was characterized by progress of the East-West negotiations that brought the SALT talks to a conclusion on May 1, 1972; by the fundamental treaty between the two Germanies in December 1972; by the beginning of negotiations in Vienna for the reduction of forces in Europe; and by the beginning of negotiations in Helsinki on cooperation and security in Europe during the first half of 1973. The Socialists, who had focused on the end of tensions in Europe, were satisfied by these developments, while the Social Democrats were cautious. In a Chamber of Deputies debate on September 27, 1973, on dissent in the USSR and detente, the PSDI asked for preliminary "indications by the Soviets of their acceptance of the principle and practice of free circulation of men and ideas" (intervention of Hon. Cariglia).

Beyond the European context, the policy of equidistance and adherence to the resolutions of the United Nations (which Moro, the Foreign Minister of the last center-left government had adopted with regard to the Middle East) met the consensus of the two socialist parties. The Yom Kippur War and its serious consequences made evident new difficulties between the two parties. The PSDI, more pro-Israel and pro-American, criticized the Syrian-Egyptian attack, and was undecided over the outcome of the Palestinian problem. The PSI, instead, shared the position taken by the government in the days of the crisis, insofar as they made reference to multilateral initiatives (UN and EEC) to which Italy had to contribute. The PSI, moreover, struggled within the government to have the Palestinian problem dealt with on political and national terms.

It was Vietnam, however, during the early '70s, that highlighted the differences in international policy between the PSI and the PSDI and the other center-left parties. To the PSDI and the Italian government's cautious dissociation from the American ally, the PSI posed a more incisive and antonomous action. The Socialist leaders' criticism, while the party was in the government, was tied to opportunistic considerations. Throughout the country, however, mainly because of an initiative by the Lombardi group, the PSI was again lined up with the rest of the left, notably with the PCI, espousing once again the common themes of antiimperialism and international solidarity. In Parliament the alignment with the left became evident during the debate about diplomatic recognition of North Vietnam (March 1973) while the PSI was not in the government. Communists and Socialists, on that occasion, asked that recognition be extended also to the Revolutionary and Provisional Government of South Vietnam. This request was rejected by Foreign Minister Medici.

The Chilean coup d'etat in September prolonged, at the end of 1973, the antiimperialist alignment of the PSI with the PCI; but then the PSI was again in the government and the Christian Democrats participated in the protest against the end of democracy in the Latin American country.

The early '70s also saw a worsening of the Italian economic situation in connection with the crisis that struck the international monetary system (suspension of the convertibility and devaluation of the dollar in 1971; attempts by the IMF to find a new system of regulating exchanges). The crisis of Italian exports brought to light the competitive limitations of Italian products. In addition to technical problems,[17] important political problems developed concerning relations to be initiated or reinforced in order to guarantee a framework of commercial exchanges. The inability to have the Community approve the relationship between monetary and economic policies and the difficulty in establishing decisive contacts with the Arab and Mediterranean countries became political problems that the Socialists had to face, sometimes without an adequate analysis of the situation at hand.

THE EUROSTRATEGY (1974–77)

In fact, the debate developed under pressure of the economic crisis that worsened after 1973 and while the internal political scene experienced tensions and changes. Within the Social Democratic Party, during these last years, the international themes were absent from internal discussions. The PSDI went through a period of serious crises and changes in leadership. The Social Democrats have almost completely lost contact with their European brother parties. An intense revival of international connections (which will be evaluated in the future), has become, instead, a characteristic of the new party secretariat after the nomination of Romita as secretary.

On the other hand, the scarcity of international contacts also characterized the PSI of De Martino, when the party was more concerned with the internal situation and the elaboration of foreign policy themes was quite reduced. The connection with the PCI on antiimperialism and solidarity was particularly defended by the Lombardi group, which was the strongest opponent of the Socialist International. The left wing of the party studied in depth the themes of the crisis of the international economy in terms of relations between industrial countries and developing countries and not simply on the technical level of trade and of the increase of petroleum prices. Besides, from this analysis derived the strategic perspective of the alternative of the left and of the alliance with the communist parties of Western Europe, to which the Socialist International was opposed. The majority of the party, however, sided with positions of autonomy and with the PCI only on certain matters of foreign policy.[18] To this the party leaders added, as a matter of special significance, the connection with other European socialist parties. The advance of the socialists in other European countries (France, Portugal, Great Britain, the Federal Republic of Germany) contributed to the making of this choice; but the search for solutions to the crisis of the economic system of the industrial states was also a determining factor. This search also sought for solutions to national crises of states such as Great Britain, Portugal, and Italy, where the socialists are in the government or near the area of government, solutions that in great part depend upon the economic policy of the Federal Republic of Germany where a socialist party is also in the government. Thus, in an increasing series of encounters, Eurosocialism was born as an attempt to realize substantial and programmatic accords. The reality of very different national situations is, however, an important factor and one that predominates over other considerations.

The new party secretary, Craxi, has taken Eurosocialism as a strategic and programmatic party line to be realized mainly inside the European Community. The PSI is, together with the German SPD, unconditionally favorable to elections by universal and direct vote for the European Parliament and looks for the issuance of a common programmatic declaration. Besides participating in every meeting of all the European Socialist and Social Democratic parties, Craxi has had direct contacts with the Socialist leaders of the Community, such as Brandt, Schmidt, Callaghan, and Mitterand (September, October 1976). Giolitti is now part of the Commission of the Community. However, the EEC's problems (regional fund, common economic policy, extension to other southern European countries, agricultural policy, and so on) are difficult to resolve and the socialists of the various states are not in agreement on the solutions to be adopted. Within the same Italian Socialist party there are different attitudes and concepts of the EEC. Many party sectors are more than anything else influenced by the Community's democratic problems and by the prospects of a "People's Europe." The nomination of Giolitti as Commissioner, an economic technocrat, showed, nevertheless, that attention is given to the monetary problems of the Community. On the other hand, Giolitti represents the majority attitude of the party leadership toward the EEC; that is, the support of the potential of the existing institutions and the prospect of greater adherence to socialist principles. However, the left wing of the party, which has never completely accepted the Community "as it is," keeps criticizing the capitalist character of the EEC structures and its secondary role with regard to American imperialism and asked for the abandonment of these features of the Community.

The relationship with other European socialist parties, which dominates the communitarian thematic, is also to be found in the thematic of pan-European relations. The subjects of cooperation and European security were debated at the Socialist International in view of the Belgrade Conference. But after the signing of the Helsinki Convention, the interest given to these subjects within the PSI has not been very great. In reality, the attention paid to international affairs has been discontinuous, limited, and hardly diffused throughout the party base, which is almost never called upon to face matters of international and foreign policy.[19] In this lack of debate on foreign policy, finally, one should note the little attention given to the Mediterranean question. The party, thanks mainly to left-wing initiatives, has often protested the military presence in the Mediterranean of the great powers; but, together with this, mention must be made of the strong criticism toward certain Christian Democratic initiatives concerning the Mediterranean, including accusations of third-force leanings. The Mediterranean question does not seem to be dealt with in proper terms or with sufficient attention. Thus it is not surprising that the socialists, in spite of an undisputed solidarity with third-world countries, have only of late become a part in the debate on relations between Europe and the Mediterranean area. Recently, the subject of the attraction and integration of Italy to continental Europe has been overshadowed by the consideration of a possible Italian role as intermediary between central and northern Europe on one side and southern Europe and the Mediterranean-African world on the other.

NOTES

1. See DOXA poll cited by L. Graziano, *Italian Foreign Policy in the Post War* (Padova: Marsilio, 1968), p. 49.

2. It must be kept in mind, particularly to understand the evolutions of the two party lines, that the leadership of each party was divided on matters of international policy. In the PSLI the pro-West position of the Saragat group (which was always in the majority), differed from the genuinely neutralist position of Mondolfo. In the PSI the Nenni and Morandi pro-Soviet currents clashed with fundamentally neutralist currents headed by Lombardi and Jacometti, which held the party majority for only a short time.

3. See quotation "Declaration on the party international policy" issued by the Secretariat on October 1, 1948.

4. Romita's current view, which did not accept this unity, in fact left the party on the occasion of the 28th Congress (May 1949). Concerning the internal debate of the Socialist

Party for the ratification of the Atlantic Pact, see D. Ardia, *The Socialist Party and The Atlantic Pact* (Milan: Angeli, 1976).

5. On the national ideals of the PSI in the 1950s, see A. Benzoni and V. Tedesco, *The Socialist Movement in the Post War* (Padova: Marsilio, 1968), pp. 74–76.

6. On pacifism of the PSI see A. Benzoni, *The Socialists and Foreign Policy*, in IAI, *The Foreign Policy of the Italian Republic* (Milan: Comunita, 1967), pp. 931–32.

7. The change in direction happened at the 32nd party Congress in Venice (February 6–10, 1957) that marked the break between Nenni's autonomists and Lombardi's left against anti-Soviet "excommunications," and it became stronger at the 33rd Congress in Naples (January 15–19, 1959).

8. The PSI abstained from voting the EEC treaty and voted favorably for EURATOM.

9. In two articles in *Avanti* of May 4 and 21, 1958.

10. Socialist motion in the Chamber for disarmament and the creation of a neutral zone in central Europe (February 5, 1958).

11. A sector of the party left wing remained pro-Soviet; Basso, Vecchietti, etc.

12. N. Kogan, *Italian Foreign Policy* (Milan: Lerici, 1965), p. 173.

13. Reunion of the party central committee and Nenni's article in *Foreign Affairs*.

14. Even after the schism of the PSIUP, there were always some members, such as Lombardi, for whom the acceptance of NATO was necessary only because of certain circumstances that definitely annulled the option of a neutralist basis.

15. A. Coppola, *Moro* (Milan: Feltrinelli, 1976), p. 50.

16. This opinion is also shared by scholars and socialist politicians such as Benzoni (loc. cit.), and G. Tamburrano, *History and Chronicle of the Center-Left* (Milan: Feltrinelli, 1976).

17. The Socialist Minister of Trade, Zagari, had delineated in 1970–71 the hypothesis (never realized) of a bank for operations of financing and credits for export.

18. "The Socialist International, which supposedly should mediate between the European Socialist parties and the Social Democratic parties, reveals once more its uselessness"; M. Achilli, "The Alternative and Reflections on International Policy," in *The Socialist Alternative*, ed. M. Achilli and F. Dambrosio (Milan Mazzotta, 1976), pp. 46–56.

19. See paragraph on PSI political culture in G. Are, *Italy and International Changes 1971–1976* (Florence: Valecchi, 1977).

CHAPTER

8

THE PORTUGUESE SOCIALISTS: RESTRUCTURING PORTUGUESE FOREIGN POLICY

Thomas C. Bruneau

The specific purpose of this chapter is to analyze the foreign policy positions of the Socialist (PS) government formed in July 1976 as the first constitutional government of the third Portuguese Republic. The analysis will range much further, however, as nine months is too brief a period and the Socialists' initiatives cannot be appreciated without extensive background. This background will include aspects of previous Portuguese foreign policy, policies of other governments and institutions, and internal regime characteristics—all of which are interrelated in this case. The Portuguese experience runs counter to much "established wisdom" on the relationships between external factors and internal characteristics. It does not fit the Prague model, although advocated by some and feared by many others, nor does it approximate the Cuban pattern, thereby probably avoiding the former. It clearly contradicts the Chilean experience of 1973 regarding the behavior of most external actors and the military (although some of those defeated by the alliance of the PS and "the moderates" in the MFA [Armed Forces Movement] may not appreciate this), and the poignant film on the fall of Allende, "il Pleut Sur Santiago," has been showing in Lisbon for six months.

The processes of regime formation and elaboration of foreign policy continue; however, based on what has taken place so far the Portuguese experience is clearly important. For Portugal internally it means the end of a half century of de facto dictatorship and structures of class repression in which the only real option for social mobility was emigration. Externally it represents the demise of an empire that was the third largest in the colonial era, being more than 20 times the size of metropolitan

Portugal itself. The transformation of these internal and external characteristics, and the manner in which they were transformed, included revolutionary processes, and the restructuring, as well as search for a new role, has involved external actors. These actors (including governments, parties, unions, and other groups) became involved because of the timing and potential extent of Portuguese developments. The revolutionary aspects began at the same period as the fall of the Greek junta (July 1974), when changes were expected with the anticipated death of Franco (fall 1975), as the French Socialists and Communists were cooperating in the Common Program, and the Italian Communists increasing in electoral strength. Portuguese events, therefore, were dramatic and far-reaching in scope with potential implications for Southern Africa, Europe, and East-West relations because of Portugal's location and its membership in NATO. Portugal has thus attracted wide foreign attention and involvement; the current foreign policies of the PS government which came to power as a function of this involvement must be appreciated in this light.

In analyzing the Portuguese case I have drawn upon the relevant literature in the discipline of International Relations—that which falls within the rubric of the "penetration" approach. The approach emphasizes that systems are penetrated when external actors of various types and varying intentions play significant roles in domestic politics. The literature is rich in insights and encourages a certain perception that was not fostered in the traditional literature on state behavior, but at this point in its development is extremely general and even vague. As its foremost proponent lamented in a recent article: there has been no theoretical breakthrough and the common pattern is to employ new rhetoric to analyze old problems.[1] In this study I employ the useful insights from the literature and thereby not only analyze the evidence as effectively as possible but also contribute material whereby the approach itself may be further elaborated. It will be shown that Portugal is penetrated and this is in fact desired by some domestic elites. Probably a better term is "linked" and Rosenau notes that the terms are used as synonyms. This linkage is discussed and it will be demonstrated how the foreign policies of the PS government are intended to increase and strengthen the links in order to remain in power and secure the liberal democratic regime that is currently being formulated.[2]

The conservative-authoritarian regime—the Estado Novo—that Oliveira Salazar fashioned and directed (1928–68) was intended to maintain in Portugal a glorified traditional order of hardworking peasants and worthy lords. It was consciously antiparliamentary, antidemocratic, and antiliberal and was formally structured according to corporatist ideas of representation. The political system was explicitly structured to be autonomous from society and the country socially and economically isolated from the rest of the world. Oliveira Salazar did not want Portugal to industrialize for he feared a strong Socialist movement would inevitably follow. Contacts of all types, therefore, were minimized and the linkages between Portugal and the rest of the world were as slight as possible.[3] This political system had much in common with those of Spain and Italy and, to a certain degree, with Nazi Germany. When the latter two were defeated in the Second World War there was general anticipation that the regimes of Franco and Oliveira Salazar would soon follow because of their isolation and the unpopularity of fascism. Portugal received better treatment than Spain after the war in part because of the agreement that allowed the Allies to use the Azores for air and naval bases.

Portugal was invited in 1949 to be one of the eleven original members of the Atlantic Alliance and Oliveira Salazar profited more directly than Franco from the anticommunist aspects of NATO. He used the Atlantic Pact in a very selective manner. Neglecting the democratic tenor in the preamble he drew support from the anticommunist reality to sustain himself and the regime. In continuing to minimize contacts he emphasized the political and military suport and generally refused the economic aid offered through the Marshall Plan.[4] Portugal's active contribution to NATO was slight. Although an army division was promised for NATO use in 1952 it never materialized, and the main coordination was with the Portuguese Navy in maneuvers. Undoubtedly the main contribution, in exchange for the support, was the use by NATO of port and communications facilities in Portugal and by the United States of Lajes Field in the Azores.

When guerrilla warfare erupted in the African colonies in 1961, Oliveira Salazar utilized the Atlantic Alliance designed for the North Atlantic for the retention of colonies in the Southern Hemisphere. There were fluctuations and certainly dissimulations in the policies of NATO and its members regarding Portugal's wars but generally the most important members, including the United States and Germany, were supportive of Portugal's continuation in Africa. Germany and France supplied war materials, and the United States granted substantial financial aid after 1972.[5] Thus through a relatively low level of penetration by NATO, Oliveira Salazar received substantial support to keep himself and his regime in power and Portugal in Africa.

Not even NATO support was sufficient for Portugal to maintain its former high level of economic autonomy and pursue three simultaneous guerrilla wars in Africa. The commitment of 11.2 percent of men of military age for the regular armed forces was the second highest in the world (Israel is first), and the military portion of the national budget was approximately 45 percent, which gave Portugal with 7.5 percent the highest ratio of defense expenditures to GNP in the world. Salazar was forced to reverse his longstanding policies of economic isolation, and legislation in 1965 was changed to encourage foreign investment and trade in Portugal and the colonies. The new policies and the encouragement of tourism were effective and Portugal became fully integrated into world patterns of investment and trade. Whereas the foreign share of Portuguese industry in 1960 was only 1.5 percent, by 1970 it was some 27 percent. There was a flood of foreign investment into the colonies as well, with the largest corporations such as Gulf Oil and Krupp leading the way.[6] Portugal's trading patterns evolved accordingly, and, paradoxically, while the goal of intensifying foreign investment and trade was to secure Portuguese control in Africa, the colonial portion of trade decreased substantially. This is not to imply that the colonial trade was unimportant, for much was in protected markets, there were extensive hidden transfers, and the colonies assisted in balancing Portugal's trade deficits. The striking fact is the reorientation of trade, for while the exports to the colonies in 1964 were 25 percent of the total and imports 15 percent, by 1974 these figures had decreased to 11 percent and 10.5 percent respectively.

Following Salazar's debilitating stroke in 1968, Marcello Caetano took office and assumed an initially liberalizing stance that suggested there would be a conscious reorientation of the economy towards Europe as well as changes within Portugal and its relationship with Africa. This clearly did not happen, as evidenced by the facts that the "ultra" President Américo Thomaz was reimposed in 1972, discussion of the issue of Africa was prohibited in the campaign for the National Assembly in 1973, and censorship as well as repression increased. Economic processes did not lead to political changes but rather caused reactions. In the failure to innovate, Portugal entered into a process that must be termed a general crisis of economy and society. Inflation increased from 5 percent in 1967 to 16 percent in 1971, to 20 percent in 1973, and the economy was stagnating as foreign investment dropped off. The population actually decreased by 180,000 between 1960 and 1970, and a general sense of frustration and anxiety was manifest as illegal strikes and violence increased. It could be argued that there was no change in the internal or foreign policies because of the greater strength of the economic interests in Africa vs. those in Europe. Yet both Portuguese corporations and the foreign ones were essentially the same and, if anything, the foreigners would probably have an easier time dealing with Angola and Mozambique if these states were independent or at least more autonomous. The answer must be found instead in the ideological commitment of Oliveira Salazar as cemented into an alliance of military and civilian groups committed to maintaining Portugal in Africa for their continued rule. Whether Portugal can survive without the colonies will be clear in short order, but by 1974 it was evident that the country could not pursue antiguerrilla warfare on three simultaneous fronts.[7]

It was most evident to those who were closest to fighting the wars; that is, the middle officers at the rank of captain or major who had responsibility for leading the troops in the field. An abundance of literature has been published on the coup and this is not the place to summarize it. The main points are the following: these officers realized through their own experience in the field that the wars could not be won militarily; they had ample evidence to think they would be held responsible for a tragedy that was due to political leadership in Lisbon; they knew from the experience of General Spinola in attempting to convince Marcelo Caetano and the reactions to the publication of his book—*Portugal and the Future*—that there would be no political solution forthcoming; and the catalyst for the organization of the MFA and final triumph was the decree law 353/73 of July 1973 that provided for the entry of militia recruits to the officers corps. So far there has been no evidence that foreign governments were aware of, let alone involved in, the coup of 25 April 1974.[8]

The program of the MFA clearly stated that the main priority of the coup was to end the wars as quickly as possible. The program also indicated that Portugal would continue to honor its international commitments. There was much in the program, which was a good indicator of the feelings of the principal actors at the time, and it provided for democratic government, eventual return of the military to an exclusive defense role, a better situation for the lower classes, and other positive features. The members of the MFA were, by and large, politically untutored and relied on various platforms and statements from political parties in preparing the program. There were only the slightest hints in the program of the kinds of changes and processes that would be unleashed in Portugal during the ensuing two years. These hints are found in the option for improving the lot of the lower classes by "means of an antimonopoly strategy." This can be read as either anticapitalist or anti-the particular form of monopolization of the Portuguese economy by a handful of companies. The best explanation for the fulfillment of this particular line of the program (to the detriment of others) and the rapid structural changes that were involved in it can be found in two interacting processes—the selection of General Spinola as head of Junta of National Salvation (JSN) and subsequently as Provisional President and the frenetic formation of political parties of all sizes and orientations.

Both of these processes have been previously discussed and it is necessary here to reiterate only the basics.[9] General Spinola had indicated at least two years before the coup that he wanted to rule and his book—*Portugal and the Future*—described the orientations he would take. If he had his way there would be increased autonomy rather than independence for the colonies, a limited degree of political liberalization at home, and restricted socioeconomic changes. This would amount to what Kenneth Maxwell has called "a liberal revolution."[10] Spinola was considered safe by Western leaders and reassured President Nixon whom he met in June 1974 in the Azores. Through his appointments in the Provisional government, relations with center and rightist parties, and attempts to secure control of the armed forces he sought to implement these policies. However, his actions and policies made the MFA increasingly aware that their as yet undefined goals were in opposition to those of the General. Thus occurred a complex and at times contradictory process: as General Spinola attempted to implement his plans, the MFA saw itself in opposition and defined a more radical position. At each stage of the conflict between General Spinola and the MFA—from July 1974 until 11 March 1975—the radicalization of the MFA and of the revolutionary process itself was pushed ahead.

The program of the MFA provided for associations and not parties. Immediately after the coup, however, numerous parties formed and the MFA—not in direct control at this point—had to recognize a fait accompli. As parties were illegal under the Estado Novo, the only fully formed party was the Communist (PCP) which had existed clandestinely since 1926. As the MFA was pushed further to the left in its conflict with General Spinola and his supporters, its members found themselves approximating the PCP both ideologically and organizationally. As other parties formed and the political struggle escalated from about July 1974, there was a widespread radicalization to keep pace with the MFA and a momentum was established. The MFA still did not have a tutelary role well defined, let alone secured, and virtually every aspect of polity, society, and economy became an issue in the political struggle. In the process of radicalization from roughly September 1974 until the high point in July 1975 the country did, in fact, experience a revolutionary process of change. The African colonies either became independent or had the dates specified for same; there were threats of independence in the Azores and Madeira; banks and insurance companies were nationalized, along with other businesses and industries, so that the state's share of investment increased from 18 percent to 45 percent; 1,300 large properties were taken over; and a large but undetermined number of businesses were put under worker control. These processes lacked an overall plan, for they were largely the result of a power struggle between individuals and groups; however, the structural changes deserve the term revolutionary even if without a central direction or plan.

Yet there were a number of plans offered and even partially implemented. The most consistent military thinker and guiding light in terms of models has been Major Melo Antunes. His ideas as indicated in the Political, Social, and Economic Program (21 February 1975), the Political Action Plan (21 June 1975), and in his interviews seek, in my view, a reasonable transformation of Portuguese society and the diversification of Portuguese relations abroad. During his period of prominence Portugal established or reestablished diplomatic relations with the Soviet Union, Eastern Europe, India, and countries in the Middle East and Africa. His plans were oriented to a certain type of Third Worldism in which Portugal would serve as a bridge or liaison between Europe and the less developed parts of the world. By April 1975 his plans and group were superseded by more radical plans and groups advocating either an Eastern European model such as that of Premier Vasco Gonçalves and the PCP or an Asian model such as the Alliance of the People—MFA (8 July 1975). In sum, Portugal was undergoing a revolutionary change in regard to foreign dependencies, internal structures, and processes, and several somewhat contradictory plans were advanced to integrate everything. As these plans and processes included both internal regime characteristics and foreign policy, they of necessity concerned foreign governments. Portugal thus attracted much international attention and involvement and the subsequent resolution of the Portuguese revolution and its foreign role is best understood along two analytical lines: 1) the international context in an era of detente, and 2) the particular configuration of power in Portugal.

1. The high points of the Portuguese revolution occurred during the same period as the Vladivostok meeting between Brezhnev and Ford (November 1974) and the Helsinki Conference (August 1975). The United States and other NATO members were upset by the presence of Communists in the Portuguese cabinets and with the increasing role of the PCP and groups further to the left in important sectors of the government and society. It seemed a second Cuba, with communist takeover of a political movement initiated by noncommunist elements but with greater implications for strategy as well as detente. With the Soviet Navy expanding in the Mediterranean and the Indian Ocean, and the possibility that it would receive special privileges in Southern Africa and possibly the same in Portugal and the Azores, the implications for defense strategy were serious indeed. The United States emphasized publicly that it was concerned with the events and President Ford reminded Brezhnev in Vladivostok that Portugal was in the West, yet later stated that Portugal might have to withdraw from NATO.[11] The Soviet Union faced a dilemma. In favor of heavy and obvious support for a Cuban pattern were strategic considerations and the fact that the PCP was in an even more favorable position than the PSP had been in Cuba. If it worked it would

also be a lesson to the Eurocommunists not to stray too far from orthodoxy. However, there were as many factors against following a Cuban pattern: Cuba itself has been expensive and there was no reason to believe that Portugal would be any less so; the PCP did hold a great deal of power but always as a function of its relations with elements in the armed forces and these individually and jointly were unpredictable; it would undoubtedly mean the end of detente as the United States made its position clear on the importance of the case; and it probably could not work anyway given Portugal's location and the commitment of the United States and other NATO countries that could assist rightist groups in Spain and Portugal.[12] Whereas Cuba could be termed a Soviet success, Chile was anything but, and Portugal was more likely to become the latter rather than the former. Thus the Soviet Union supported, and continues to support, the PCP in the media and through aid. But it emphasized that this support did not extend to the point of the PCP taking full power and implementing an East European model of economy and society. The evidence for this cautionary strategy is abundant and extends from Edward Gierek's advice for moderation in Lisbon in January 1975, to President Podgorny's advice to President Costa Gomes in Moscow in October 1975 to do the same, and the notice from Soviet Ambassador Kalinin to Vasco Gonçalves that there would be no confrontation between the USSR and the United States over Portugal. Ambassador Kalinin (who had previously been in Cuba) also informed the U.S. Ambassador, Carlucci, that he had made his position clear on this matter.[13] There was, therefore, no feasible way Portugal could adopt the more radical plans put forth and already followed to some degree. In this sense Portugal is penetrated as the superpowers set the conditions for what is ultimately possible or impossible.

2. The particular manner whereby the internal configuration emerged in Portugal is important both for the country itself and for aiding our understanding of penetration or linkage. The pattern of U.S.-USSR relations and understandings concerning Portugal did not in itself determine the particular political and social system being formed. The unfeasibility of a radical pattern did not necessitate a liberal democratic model, as a military or civilian rightist pattern was, and still is, possible. The particular evolution is due to the interaction of both internal and external factors. Internally it must be noted again that the PCP had substantial power only as a function of its relationship to the armed forces. There was no conscious agreement within the armed forces concerning particular models or strategies and individuals were influenced by the models promoted by political parties and groups. The East European approach supported by Vasco Gonçalves was but one—albeit predominant—for the period of March to September 1975. The group that formed to oppose this

pattern—The Nine—was led by Major Melo Antunes and was motivated to do so for a variety of reasons. Personally the officers would lose influence if the orientation promoted by Vasco Gonçalves won and the military as institution would probably be so polarized and fragmented that their power base would disappear as well. This was dramatized by the attempted subversion of the commando regiment at Amadora on 31 July 1975 when PCP militants promoted a mutiny against the commander, Colonel Jaime Neves, involved with The Nine. This was after the Républica affair that was an attempt to silence the main organ of the PS and took place as anticommunist violence was increasing in the North.[14] It is of utmost importance to realize that other political options existed beyond the PCP. In terms of organization and militancy the PS did not compare with the PCP and thus had been disadvantaged from the beginning. It did, however, receive the greatest percentage of the votes in the elections for the Constituent Assembly on 25 April 1975 and thus could make a claim to have an important voice in government (38 percent vs. 26 percent PPD and 13 percent PCP). Yet the question was precisely over what type of regime Portugal was to have, and votes were not accepted as a valid indicator by the PCP and its supporters in the armed forces. In opposing Vasco Gonçalves, The Nine tended to develop an alliance with the PS and thereby provided a basis for a liberal democratic system.

Further motivation was provided for The Nine by external actors. They were aware of the concern of the United States and NATO as well as the limits on aid from the USSR. It was also emphasized that the United States, individual European states, and the EC would not grant loans unless a liberal democratic political system was established in Portugal. After 50 years of rightist isolation Portugal was now to be intentionally isolated by the West for its leftism. There was a certain degree of coordination of this strategy of isolation by the Socialists in Western Europe, the PS, and the Americans. The fact that the PS could offer an option was due in large part to the Socialists of Europe (Social Democrats in fact), and particularly the SPD. The PS itself had been founded in Western Germany in 1973 with assistance from the Friedrich Ebert Foundation and contacts were extremely close with the Germans and the Swedes. These parties supplied various types of resources to assist the development of the PS, including funds (but probably not more than the USSR for the PCP), technical know-how, strategy, and obvious and intense public support both in Portugal and outside. It is also worth noting that the PCP was held in disrepute by the Eurocommunists in France, Italy, and Spain and they too supported the PS in statements. It must be emphasized that despite its newness the PS was an authentic party—at least as authentic as the PCP but organizationally weaker. It built on a long history of socialist thought in Portugal, its cadre had been involved in politics before and had suffered, and they attempted to organize while in exile. Thus the context was defined by the detente between the United States and the Soviet Union, but the particular manner of resolution was the interaction between military (The Nine) and civilian (PS) groups within Portugal who were influenced and linked with mainly European parties.

The outcome of the interaction was that The Nine, in conjunction with the PS and other parties to its right, forced out Vasco Gonçalves, formed another Provisional Government (the Sixth) composed of elements of The Nine, the PS, PPD, and token PCP representation, and moderated the revolution. This remained tentative, however, as the proponents of a more radical aproach to political change in the armed forces and the parties were still active in developing strategies to regain power. During the fall of 1975 there was a continual struggle between The Nine-PS alliance and groups further to the left that culminated in an attempted leftist coup on 25 November. This coup had been anticipated and was put down very quickly, mainly by Jaime Neves' commandos. This led to a purging of the left within the armed forces and a limiting of the PCP and more leftist parties for lack of military allies. It also opened the way for the particular political evolution that has been followed ever since.

In most senses The Nine represent the original line of the program of the MFA (and generally consist of a core of the same individuals) and are supervising a limited retreat of the armed forces from direct political involvement. In this regard they promoted the elections for the Legislative Assembly in April 1976, the Presidency in June, and local levels in December. Thus far they have advocated the forms and supervised the processes whereby a liberal democratic system can be established in Portugal. In the elections to the Legislative Assembly on 25 April 1976 the PS won 35 percent (vs. 24 percent PPD, 14 percent PCP, and 16 percent CDS), thus obtaining a plurality of 106 seats out of 261. Despite the moderate margin over its opposition, the PS decided to govern alone and ruled out alliances either to the left—with the PCP—or the right—with the PPD. In the presidential elections of June the candidate of The Nine, the PS, PPD, and CDS—General Ramalho Eanes—received 61 percent of the vote (vs. 16 percent for Otelo Saraiva de Carvalho, his closest competitor). The political system in which they operate is sui generis and reflects the concern of The Nine, who would prefer to remain apart from politics yet fear that the lack of democratic experience in Portugal, combined with the severe difficulties that face the country, may overwhelm a civilian government, especially a minority one. The system is based on the constitution written by representatives elected on 25 April 1975 and includes a Platform of Accord signed by The Nine and the six main parties on 26 February 1976. The resultant system cannot be modified for the duration of the first government under the constitution—four years—and then only by a two-thirds majority. The system is semipresidential and semimilitary. The president holds extensive powers to form or dissolve a government, promulgate and decree laws, and to declare war and a state of siege. He is not obligated to use these powers fully but they are there if he decides to employ them.[15] The president and government are in turn supervised by the Revolutionary Council (CR) which is selected from within the armed forces and dominated by The Nine. The CR has extensive powers to guide the president (who presides in the CR), to supervise the government, and to judge on the constitutionality of legislation. Portugal clearly is not a typical liberal democracy, for the government is supervised and controlled, but can be if the government can govern and provide peace and stability.

There is reason to doubt the capacity of the PS government to govern in peace and stability. As a minority government it is limited and encounters obstacles in passing legislation to confront the crises facing the country. On the left is the strong PCP and a variety of more radical groups. On the right is the PPD-PSD and the CDS further to the right. In the local elections of December 1976, the PS received 33 percent of the votes (vs. 25 percent for the PPD-PSD, 17 percent for the PCP coalition, and 16 percent for the CDS), and thus cannot claim it has anything approaching a mandate to take extremely difficult measures. Beyond the political-party arena, the PS does not control important groups and associations such as the unions (mainly aligned with the PCP), the Confederation of Portuguese Industries (more in sympathy with the PPD-PSD), or the Confederation of Portuguese Agriculturalists (in sympathy with the PPD-PSD or more to the right). This is not to mention the various clandestine groups (left and right) opposed to the survival of a liberal democratic regime under any kind of party control. There is much sense to the supervisory role of the president and the CR, but there is real danger if the composition of the latter shifts; or if the president falls out of sympathy with the CR or the government the democratic form could be rapidly terminated. Then, too, since there is power in the CR it provides an important role for continued politicization of the armed forces. There are, then, a number of obvious problems in the political system, and while these might not be serious in an established system (although one cannot imagine these features there) they are in the unstable and difficult Portuguese case.

The country is undergoing economic and social crises. It was facing similar problems before the coup and, as they were due largely to the commitment to remain in Africa, the coup was the solution at the political level. The crises have not been resolved by the subsequent three years of revolutionary activity and in some respects have been exacerbated.

Decolonization was disorganized and the civil war in Angola has left Portugal with the legacy of more than half a million refugees who have bleak futures. These people can provide the basis for rightist movements—both legal and clandestine—and present an almost insurmountable problem for any government in a time of world economic contraction when the possibility of emigration is limited. The economic crisis is more serious now than it was at the time of the coup, for the reserves of some $2.5 billion are almost gone and the country can no longer rely on the hidden transfers from the colonies, the protected markets, and the guaranteed supplies in goods such as petroleum, sugar, and coffee. Inflation is somewhat less but still running at 20 percent, unemployment is conservatively estimated at 15 percent, and there is a massive balance-of-payments deficit. In the first half of 1976 exports covered only 40 percent of imports with a resultant deficit of $1.2 billion. Portugal has traditionally run deficits but these were balanced by income from the colonies, emigrants' remittances, and tourism. Remittances in 1976 were 10 percent less than in 1973 and tourism was some 60 percent less. There are limitations in how far the deficit can be reduced, for much of it is in petroleum and food. In 1975 petroleum composed 14 percent of total imports. Portugal produces only 40 percent of its agricultural consumption and is the South European country running the greatest deficit. There is no doubt that the economic situation is parlous and all indicators show that its improvement will be extremely difficult.[16]

The government is fully aware of the social and economic crises and is attempting to implement austerity measures as well as rationalize the revolutionary changes that were implemented with a greater or lesser degree of planning. There are cases of denationalization, some 100 agricultural properties have been returned to their legal owners, and now a General Plan has been passed to coordinate and rationalize these measures. The dilemma is that after 50 years of repressive government and wage policies the lower classes benefited from the revolution, and it has been a nonviolent revolution in large part because of the accumulated reserves. Now, in order to implement austerity measures and rationalize changes some of the gains will be threatened and workers and peasants could throw support to the PCP and populistic groups that promise to guarantee their interests. The PS government, therefore, is supervised by the President and the CR, is opposed forcefully on the right and the left, and all this is taking place in a context of crises. It is in this predicament and in light of the manner in which the PS came to be the government that the foreign policies must be understood.

The foreign policies of this first constitutional government are extremely important as Portugal, for the first time in almost 600 years, is not an imperial power. The previous provisional governments oversaw the dissolution of the empire but, as noted above, posed contradictory models of regimes and foreign policies. It is for this present government as long as it survives, and its foreign policies are intricately related to its survival, to define Portugal's new role or mission in the world. The main orientations of the government in foreign policy (and everything else) can be found in its program presented to the nation by Mário Soares in early August 1976 and briefly reiterated by the minister of foreign affairs, Medeiros Ferreira, at the United Nation on 7 October. The three main points emphasized are 1) to move with all haste into the closest possible contact with Europe—the Opção Europeia (European Option); 2) to improve and strengthen relations with Portuguese-speaking countries in Africa and with Brazil; and 3) to strengthen relations with certain priority countries, for example, Venezuela and the Middle East.

The PS government places tremendous emphasis on integration with Europe as quickly and as thoroughly as possible. This is at variance not only with the radical options posed during the past three years, but also contradicts the moderate policy of Major Melo Antunes as both a key MFA figure and minister of foreign affairs between March 1975 and the taking of power of the current government in July 1976. Melo Antunes promoted a diversification of relations in order to maximize the autonomy of Portugal, and although a certain prominence was granted to Europe this was not emphasized. When in Brussels in late January 1976, for instance, he indicated that Portugal was in no hurry to broaden its associate status with the EC.[17] In contrast, the PS government is committed to become a full member of the EC as quickly as possible. The government has created a commission to study the strategy of full memberships and is planning a ministry for this purpose in the near future. The prime minister, Mário Soares, has visited the capitals of the Nine to prepare them for Portugal's application that was submitted on 28 March. This entry is very important and, as the focal point of all foreign policy, requires some elaboration.

Mário Soares and other prominent members of the PS were in exile in Europe and developed a number of contacts as well as affinities.[18] These contacts were of utmost importance in the particular resolution of the political regime in 1975 and the external aid provided by such personalities as Schmidt, Brandt, and Palme was matched by their appearances with the Socialists in Portugal itself. The European Option, therefore, has been formulated through the experience of the PS and the assistance of their European colleagues was crucial in their coming to power. Undoubtedly the most important reason to push for entry as a full member in the Common Market is to secure within Portugal itself the PS government and the liberal democratic regime. As the aid of the Europeans was critical in the formulation of this regime, it is believed that acceptance of the principle of Portuguese entry into the EC will deter possible threats from the left, but most certainly from the right, against the survival of a liberal democratic regime. The PS desires strong linkages in order to support itself as a party and the regime it is formulating. Its main supporters in the negotiations with the EC are the very same that were so important in the resolution of the political crisis in the summer of 1975—the Germans—and its main opponents are those that did very little—the French.

There is no overwhelming economic reason to push for full membership in the EC. While it is true that 69 percent of Portugal's exports go to the EC and EFTA, her trade balances are more positive with the latter than with the former and, on the face of it, continued membership in EFTA would seem more logical.[19] Through Portugal's membership in EFTA a free trade agreement was negotiated with the EC in 1972 that was elaborated and implemented in September 1976. The details of this agreement are the following: the elimination of EC customs duties on the import of Portuguese industrial products; a reduction in duties on fish and some farm products, and increases in the quantity of wine to be accepted; a delay in the 1972 timetable on dropping import duties on some EC industrial goods; a European Investment Bank loan of up to 200 million units of account for farm modernization projects; and the permission to transfer pensions and health benefits earned in the EC to Portugal.[20] Even though it is not a full member of the EC, Portugal has received extensive loans from it, not to mention the EFTA and the United States. The United States, in November, approved a loan of $300 million and President Ford initiated legislation whereby the United States would provide $350 million as part of a consortium with the EC for a total of $1.5 billion. The discussions on the consortium continue, but nevertheless Portugal can still benefit extensively from her membership in EFTA, her associate membership in the EC, and can negotiate loans.[21]

Full membership in the Common Market would not be possible for several years at the best. Greece applied in 1975 and is not slated for full membership until 1984 at the earliest. EC technicians counseled Portugal against full application and there are a number of problems that might not be amenable to resolution before she could join. Some of these are the free circulation of workers when Portugal has at least 15 percent unemployment and the added problem of the refugees; the competition with France and Italy for agricultural products such as wine; and the parlous state of the Portuguese economy and its low level of industrialization that might be more than the EC could tolerate. What is more, the EC is in a state of disarray, and if Portugal were to join, while Greece has already applied, Spain would most certainly follow. The EC as it has been known would surely change and quite possibly not for the better.

The explanation must be found at the political level. There are few apparent economic benefits to be derived, the chance of participating in the near future is slight, and the EC itself will have to change considerably if Portugal were to join. Most important is the point noted above: the Socialists want to have the principle of Portuguese membership accepted so as to link the country more closely with European democracies and thus deter attempts to overthrow the government and the regime. In this same perspective, Portugal became the 19th member of the Council of Europe in September 1976. As this is an assemblage of democratic countries, it demonstrated that Portugal was recognized as democratic and again provided a link whereby the regime could be further consolidated. This membership, as well as the intention to join the EC, has received extensive coverage in Portugal, thus promoting a certain image to the population as to Portugal's vocation and type of regime.[22]

The second point of Medeiros Ferreira's speech at the United Nations concerned relations with the ex-colonies in Africa and Brazil. In view of the economic disarray of Portuguese trade relations with Angola and Mozambique, from which she received 15 percent of her imports (mainly in goods such as petroleum, sugar, and coffee) in 1973 and only 3.5 percent in 1976, there is ample reason to improve these relations. Adding to this the tremendous influx of refugees that the Portuguese economy cannot possibly absorb, it becomes clear that this should be a very high priority indeed. Relations were reestablished with Angola only in late 1976, and, while some progress in negotiations is apparent, there is no immediate prospect that a substantial number of refugees can return. It is worth noting that the Opção Europeia is of such a priority that trade relations with the ex-colonies are to be negotiated in light of the Lomé Convention. Even the road to Africa is now through Europe.

Relations with Brazil must be seen in the same prism of trade relations and possible homes for the refugees. Mário Soares made an official visit to Brazil in mid-December 1976, and the main topics of discussion were possibilities to increase the miniscule trade and the relocation of more refugees beyond the 35,000 or so that have settled there during the past three years. Neither aspect is very promising, however, as Brazil is undergoing a difficult economic phase so that the trade possibilities are limited and she is unwilling to accept any but highly qualified immigrants.

The third point of the speech dealt with the strengthening of relations with certain priority countries. Since Portugal can no longer rely on supplies of petroleum based upon the production in Angola, the priority of the Middle East and Venezuela is obvious. Portugal does possess very sophisticated facilities and extensive expertise in matters related to shipbuilding and repairing and it is felt that there are possibilities to do business with the Middle East oil producers. Venezuela is seen not only as an oil producer but also as a potential investor and recipient of refugees. The President of Venezuela, Carlos Andrés Pérrez, visited Lisbon for two days in early December 1976, and a Portuguese trade mission went to Venezuela in the fall. It would appear that negotiations with Venezuela are progressing well and there is some evidence that Venezuela will attempt to arrange favorable terms for Portugal's petroleum needs.[23]

In these bilateral relations with the Portuguese-speaking countries and those of particular priority, the emphasis is upon Portugal in Europe. The end of the era of empire is being replaced with the image of Portugal as a European country, but with a special vocation in facilitating relations with the Third World. Thus something remains of Melo Antunes' notion of Portugal's place in the world but with the important difference that the first priority is Europe and then the rest of the world. The government is using this special vocation in its arguments to the EC for full membership. It is illustrated in the adherence to the Lomé Convention, in the bilateral arrangements, and was highlighted by Portugal's presence in August 1976 at Colombo for the meeting of the nonaligned nations.

The Opção Europeia is evidenced as well in Portugal's emerging role in NATO—and, as the primary reason for entering into the EC as a full member is to guarantee the government in Portugal, so it is with the new NATO role. As noted before, Portugal was an original member of the Atlantic Alliance, but its role was slight. Even during the most dynamic period of the revolution, there was no question of withdrawing from the Alliance; but the United States as well as NATO officials were preoccupied nonetheless.[24] Now that the Communists are out of the government and the PS is welcomed by the members of the Alliance, there are a number of important changes taking place. Spain and Portugal abrogated the Ibero Pact (Treaty of Friendship and Non-Aggression of 17 March 1939) in February 1976, thus freeing both from previous commitments and unpopular memories. Portugal is renegotiating the U.S. base at Lajes and the French tracking base at Flores in the Azores and is not questioning the NATO-related installations on the Continent. The relations between the Portuguese Navy and NATO have historically been the closest of any of the services, and they are being maintained through consultation, possible reequipment, and joint maneuvers. The relations with the Air Forces have been limited, but are now being increased with the provision of German jets and U.S. transports (and apparently training as well). The relations with the Army have been nominal and it is with this critical service that the changes are the greatest. In 1952 a division was promised for NATO use but never materialized. Now that Portugal is no longer fighting in Africa the armed forces are to have a total of 48,000 men (as against 110,000 in 1974) and a brigade of 3,000 is being equipped and trained by the Americans and Germans for use in NATO. This is important as a sign of Portuguese commitment to NATO, but its real significance lies in the fact of increased linkage of the most important institution in Portugal with Europe. The hope is that as the military, with NATO assistance, becomes reequipped, retrained, and involved in a new commitment, it will be less likely to exercise the political power it has held since the coup in 1974.

There is one last foreign policy initiative that should be mentioned. I have argued that the coming to power of the PS government was due in large part to the efforts of the European socialists. The leaders of the socialist movement such as Brandt and Palme have been very much in evidence in Portugal, and those who are prominent in the PS have many friends in the movement.[25] The success of socialist involvement in Portugal may well give a new lease on life to the Socialist International in assisting other socialist parties to come to power in Spain and the Third World. The PS government argues that they can serve as an intermediary in this case as well, and the visit of President Pérez of Venezuela was in part to coordinate a strategy. At the Congress of the Socialist International at Geneva in November, Mário Soares was elected as one of the vice presidents and Brandt became president. There are certain to be a number of Portuguese initiatives pursuant to its new image as a bridge, and it is reported that the PS and Spain are discussing the possibilities of a joint entry into the Common Market with the main Portuguese condition being that the Spanish Socialists—the PSOE—assume a prominent position in the regime.[26]

In this chapter a number of points have been made and the discussion has ranged far and wide; in conclusion it might be useful briefly to review the findings in light of the literature on "penetration" and "linkages." Probably what is most striking about the Estado Novo of Oliveira Salazar is the extent to which the foreign linkages were minimized, for he realized that these would decrease the autonomy of the state and thereby threaten a largely traditional society. When necessary, he selected the linkages in order to guarantee the regime, and the joining of NATO is best seen in this perspective. In the trade-off with the NATO allies Oliveira Salazar did well indeed; Portugal's active role was minimal in comparison with the political and even military support he received. This support extended to Portugal's commitment to remain in Africa even after the other members had surrendered their colonies and the United States had withdrawn from Vietnam. The tremendous demands of the wars on Portugal necessitated a reversal of trade and investment policies and Portugal drew nearer Europe as evidenced by the associated status with the EC in 1972 and the trade figures. Yet it is important to note that this reorientation did not lead to a political change, and attempts to promote new policies concerning Africa, Europe, and internal characteristics were all but eliminated by 1973. Linkages of various types, including economic, cultural, and social, do not necessarily lead to political changes. This change was brought about by a disgruntled group in the armed forces who realized the necessity of serious change in Portugal both for their own interests and for the improvement of the society. Although they agreed on the necessity of overturning the existent state they lacked a consensus on what would replace it. In the dynamic of the revolutionary processes many foreign actors were involved in promoting one or another model of the new Portuguese society and image in the world. For a period the predominant model was that promoted by the PCP and thus the United States and other members of NATO became extremely concerned and involved. The resolution of the regime took place in a context of U.S.-USSR agreement concerning the possibilities for Portugal, but the particular form that emerged is due as much to the linkages between the PS and other socialist parties. Linkage was, therefore, extremely important and remains so, for the country is undergoing crises and the foreign policy of the PS is predicated on the idea of integrating as fully and as thoroughly as possible with the European democracies. The latter, especially those in which a socialist party is important, continue to support the PS heavily and Portugal appears to be a test case for the strategy whereby socialist parties can come to power in nondemocratic regimes. The test-case aspect of Portugal is widely appreciated, and the United States has also provided large loans and is active in integrating the armed forces with NATO. Based on the Portuguese experiences during and after the Estado Novo, the particular resolution of the regime will depend on the interaction of the ideologies and competence of the political elites with the international constraints and linkages, with the latter being selected at least in part by these elites.

NOTES

1. James Rosenau, "Theorizing Across Systems: Linkage Politics Revisited," in *Conflict Behaviour and Linkage Politics*, ed. Jonathan Wilkenfeld (New York: David McKay, 1973), p. 52. For this approach see also: Karl Deutsch, "External and Internal Political Relationships," and James Rosenau, "Pre-theories and Theories of Foreign Policy," in *Approaches to Comparative and International Politics*, ed. R. Barry Farrell (Evanston, Ill.: Northwestern University Press, 1966); James Rosenau, ed., *Linkage Politics* (New York: The Free Press, 1969); Andrew M. Scott, *The Revolution in Statecraft: Informal Penetration* (New York: Random House, 1965); George Kelly and Linda Miller, "Internal War and International Systems: Perspectives on Method," in *Struggles in the State*, eds. George Kelly & Clifford Brown (New York: John Wiley, 1970). Also relevant is the literature on transnational politics and political integration. See for instance: Robert Keohane & Joseph Nye, "Transnational Relations and World Politics," *International Organization* XXV, no 3 (Summer 1971), passim., and Naomi Black, "Inside the Elephant: Intellectual Leadership in the Study of International Relations," *International Journal*, XXXI, no 4 (Autumn 1976), pp. 587–631.

2. The dependency approach that has been elaborated in Latin America and the Caribbean could be employed as well but would take us too far afield from the purpose at hand. This approach is similar to penetration but begins with economic relations and class structures rather than political relations. In the present case it could be argued that the whole evolution of Portugal is due to its dependent status with Great Britain, and Oliveira Salazar and his regime are due to this dependence. For an introduction to this literature see "Dependence and Underdevelopment in the New World and the Old," a special issue of *Social and Economic Studies*, XX, no 1 (March 1973). For the basic elements to analyze Portuguese democracy, see S. Sideri, *Trade and Power: Informal Colonialism in Anglo-Portuguese Relations* (Rotterdam: Rotterdam University Press, 1970). The problem with this approach in the Portuguese case would be to analyze the state in the Estado Novo from a class perspective, to take account of Portugal's own dependencies, to integrate the manipulation of dependency by Oliveira Salazar, and to account for changes in dependency without commensurate political changes. For a stimulating analysis of the bases of the Estado Novo see Philippe Schmitter, "The Social Origins, Economic Bases and Political Imperative of Authoritarian Rule in Portugal," in *Who Were the Fascists?* (Oslo: Universitets for laget, 1977).

3. For a detailed characterization of the regime of Oliveira Salazar see my "Portugal: Problems and Prospects in the Creation of a New Regime," *Naval War College Review*, XXIX, no. 1 (Summer 1976) and literature cited therein. A personal and comprehensive account can be found in Antonio de Figueiredo, *Portugal: Fifty Years of Dictatorship* (London: Penguin Books, 1975).

4. An extremely useful analysis of Portugal in NATO is Luc Crollen, *Portugal, the U.S. and NATO* (Leuven, Belgium: Leuven University Press, 1973). See p. 48 for the political support of NATO and pp. 90–97 for the low economic aid.

5. Ibid., pp. 125–36. See also Keith Middlemas, *Cabora Bassa: Engineering and Politics in Southern Africa* (London: Widenfeld & Nicolson, 1975) for more on these relations.

6. Crollen, pp. 108–09 and Middlemas, p. 245. There is an ample literature on foreign investment in Portugal. See for example, Maria Belmira Martins, *As multinacionais em Portugal* (Lisbon: Editorial Estampa, 1976).

7. See Middlemas for evidence on the corporations in Mozambique. For the specific political dynamics involved in the lack of reorientation see Lawrence Graham, "Portugal: The Decline and Collapse of an Authoritarian Order," *Sage Professional Papers in Comparative Politics*, vol. V, 1975, passim but particularly pp. 28, 52–55.

8. See my "Portugal: Problems and Prospects . . ." and "The Portuguese Coup: Causes and Probable Consequences," *The World Today*, XXX, no. 7 (July 1974). The best book on the coup is undoubtedly Avelino Rodrigues, et al., *O Movimento dos Capitães e o 25 de Abril* (Lisbon: Moraes, 1974).

9. "Portugal: Problems and Prospects . . ." and Avelino Rodrigues, et al., *Portugal Depois de Abril* (Lisbon: Intervoz, 1976).

10. Kenneth Maxwell, "Behind Portugal's Revolution," *New York Review of Books*, XXI, no 10 (June 13, 1974), p. 21.

11. The best general treatment of the interaction of the United States, USSR, and Portugal is Tad Szulc, "Lisbon & Washington: Behind Portugal's Revolution," *Foreign Policy*, XXI (Winter 1975–76).

12. A thinly veiled appeal for the assistance is Robert Moss, "A Ticket to Lisbon," *Harpers* (December 1975).

13. This evidence and much more is pieced together from Szulc's article, the Portuguese newspapers, and *Le Monde*. See also Jonathan Story, "Portugal's Revolution of Carnations: Patterns of Change and Continuity," *International Affairs*, LII, no. 3 (July 1976) for more analysis of this kind.

14. Szulc suggests that the CIA may have been involved in fomenting the violence in the North but is correct in deemphasizing its size or impact, p. 13. It would be an obvious strategy, but probably not necessary considering the anticommunist brainwashing of 50 years, the important role of a very conservative Church, and the fear of agrarian reform as implemented in the South. For the inside details on plotting of The Nine by a closely involved officer, see Jose Gomes Mota, *A Resistencia: O Verao quente de 1975* (Lisbon: Expresso, 1976).

15. For an analysis of the constitutional position of the President, his election, and personality see Paulino Gomes & Thomas Bruneau, *Eanes: Porque o Poder?* (Lisbon: Intervoz, 1976).

16. The most thorough and reliable data on the economic situation is found in the Annual Report of the Banco de Portugal. A quarterly publication on general economic indicators is "Conjunctura" of the Banco Portugues do Atlantico. The "Portugal-Information," which is a monthly publication of the Ministry of Mass Communication, includes frequent and useful articles on the economic situation. For analysis of the questions see the monthly journal *Economia e Socialismo.*

17. See *Expresso*, 6 August 1976, for a comparison of the policies of Melo Antunes and the program of the PS.

18. Soares' book gives a good sense of the contacts and affinities. See his *Portugal's Struggle for Liberty*, trans. by Mary Gawsworth (London: George Allen & Unwin Ltd. 1975). Also in exile were figures such as Antonio Barreto, Jorge Campinos, and Tito de Morais. There were so many that they now refer to the group of Paris, of Geneva, and so forth.

19. On the benefits of EFTA membership and the current strategy see *O Jornal*, 12 November 1976, pp. 17, 32.

20. *The London Economist*, 11 September 1976.

21. A description and analysis of earlier loans is Celso Farreira, "Ajuda externa e independencia national," *Economia e Socialismo*, 4 July 1976.

22. A fascinating comparison might be drawn between the PS intention to join the EC and thereby integrate more fully with Europe for internal political support and Cuba's admission to COMECON in 1972. In the latter case there are varying interpretations as to the initiative, but at the minimum it represents closer integration with the Soviet Union and Eastern Europe. The argument could also be made that linkages were extremely important for evolution of the Cuban regime but in this case in the era before detente. The Cuban pattern was important in Soviet calculations in Portugal and the ambassador, Arnold Kalinin, is in fact an expert on Cuba. The obverse was probably also true, for the United States could well imagine a nationalist movement being taken over by the Communist party if Soviet support was forthcoming.

23. On Pérez' trip and speculation about petroleum, see *O Jornal*, 10 December 1976, p. 6–7.

24. Joseph Luns indicated the preoccupation of NATO with Portugal in *O Jornal*, 21 May 1976. Premier Vasco Gonçalves reiterated Portugal's commitment to NATO. See his BBC interview and his speech to NATO in Vasco Gonçalves, *Discoursos* (Lisbon: Edicao Popular, 1276), pp. 46, 228–62.

25. At the PS Congress in late October there were representatives from 55 foreign parties including Brandt, Palme, Mitterand, and Kreisky.

26. *O Jornal*, 26 November 1976, p. 5.

CHAPTER

9

SOCIALISM AND WESTERN EUROPE: THE PAST

George Windell

More than a century and a quarter have passed since Karl Marx and Friedrich Engels in January 1848 published their *Manifesto of the Communist Party*, that greatest of all historical incitements to revolution. "A spectre is haunting Europe," they began, "the spectre of Communism," by which they meant a movement committed to a revolutionary overthrow of the bourgeois capitalist social order in favor of one that was to be collectivist and ultimately classless. Half a hundred pages later they closed with the thundering challenge: "The proletarians have nothing to lose but their chains. They have a world to win. WORKING MEN OF ALL COUNTRIES, UNITE!"[1] Today that spectre has been converted to reality in a large part of the world. Half of Europe is ruled by those who call themselves Communists and claim apostolic descent from Marx. Much of Asia and part of Africa are dominated by those who acknowledge Marx as their mentor. Two of the world's superpowers are so governed. Yet most of the important industrial nations of what Marx meant by Europe still think of themselves as capitalist, although, in fact, every one of them has developed a mixed economy of a sort that would have been inconceivable to him, as have two other non-European industrial giants, the United States and Japan. Workers in these nations, if they have not won the world, have in the interim acquired a great deal to lose, and it is perhaps the supreme irony that working men in communist countries where the proletarian revolution has allegedly taken place now wear the heaviest chains. Marxism, like the world of which it has become an integral part, has undergone ceaseless development in many contradictory directions since it was first articulated in 1848, and none of the versions in which it now exists is any closer to that original formulation than today's economy is to that of the mid-nineteenth century. Nor in all probability does any of them offer a less faulty analysis of today's reality—or tomorrow's—than Marx did of his.

Karl Marx,[2] born in 1818, is probably best understood as an eighteenth century *philosophe* born a generation or two late. He, and to a lesser degree, his slightly younger collaborator, Engels, believed passionately that useful knowledge would make men free and sought to give them that knowledge. Marx differed from earlier great figures of the Enlightenment such as Locke, Rousseau and even Jefferson, all of whom wrote theoretical justifications for revolution, most significantly in his conception of useful knowledge. His greatest achievement, one that has profoundly influenced the thought of nearly everyone who came later, was to focus attention upon economic activity, upon the production and distribution of goods as the basic human activity. Something so obvious ought not to have had to wait until the nineteenth century to be formulated, but it did. Marx invented neither the rich nor the poor, but he was the first to define both the bourgeoisie and the proletariat as the primary agents of social change. Class struggle presupposes consciousness of class, and Marx was certainly the first to formulate both clearly as the stuff of the historical process.[3]

Marx was a materialist, but that was also hardly anything new. He believed, however, no more than did the idealist Hegel whom, in his own view, he set on his feet,[4] or, in the view of others, on his head, that human behavior is determined by blind forces beyond the control of reason and will. Like Hegel, he described an historical process that operates through conscious rational decisions of men.[5] But because human beings must first of all eat and have shelter, material conditions associated with the production and distribution of necessities set the limits within which their rational decisions can be made. Since those conditions limit the options available, they are significant to a degree and in a way Hegel did not see, but they do not deny man the possibility of controlling his fate in the broader sense. It was the bourgeoisie that created capitalism and thereby revolutionized the world; it was not capitalism that created the bourgeoisie. Similarly, it will be, said Marx, the working class that, through conscious action, creates socialism. "The bourgeoisie, during its rule of scarce one hundred years, has created more massive and more colossal productive forces than have all preceding generations together," he wrote in the *Communist Manifesto*, and ". . . not only has the bourgeoisie forged the weapons that bring death to itself; it has called into existence the men who are to wield those weapons, the modern working class, the proletarians."[6] The operative factors are social classes made up of thinking and acting human beings, not some abstraction like "the capitalist mode of production."

While Marx was a late-blooming product of the eighteenth century Enlightenment, Marxism, as both philosophy and political movement, is more properly associated with the second half of the nineteenth century. It developed during the heyday of materialistic determinism derived from the physical sciences and from the Darwinian revolution in biology. To some, human behavior came to be as predictable as the operation of a heat engine according to the laws of thermodynamics; to others, the class struggle took on attributes analogous to the natural selection that Darwin had discerned in organic evolution. Within the Marxist movement itself, Engels was most significant in that development, for he undertook the task of interpreting Marx to others during Marx's long years of relative silence while he labored on *Capital* and especially during the 12 years that he outlived Marx. In the speech delivered at the graveside on the occasion of Marx's burial, Engels linked his colleague's philosophy of history to biological determinism. "Just as Darwin discovered the law of development of organic nature," he said, "so Marx discovered the law of development of human history."[7] In his own writings Engels later helped to convert Marx's historical materialism into its rigidly deterministic variant, dialectical materialism. History became something brought about not by human decisions, but by impersonal laws as inescapable as those that control biological evolution.[8]

This development represented both a hardening and a dehumanization of Marx's thought. Nonetheless, a great deal of his original enlightened emphasis on rational humane values did survive in western Europe into the twentieth century. He had, of course, argued in the 1848 *Communist Manifesto* that the triumph of the proletariat would require a "forcible overthrow" of the bourgeois order.[9] He reemphasized the point in his *Address of the Central Council to the Communist League* of 1850.[10] Both, however, were written under the influence of what appeared to be an imminent *bourgeois* revolution that, Marx was urging, had to be exploited for its own purposes by the proletariat. The Revolutions of 1848 failed and the revolution of 1850 did not come. As he grew older, Marx lost the heady enthusiasm of his younger days. His *Inaugural Address* to the newly founded International Working Men's Association in 1864 spoke with praise of the passage by the British Parliament of the Ten-Hour Bill: ". . . it was the first time that in broad daylight the political economy of the middle class succumbed to the political economy of the working class."[11] The success of the cooperative movement gave proof that large-scale production did not require wage labor. The proletariat must "conquer political power," but the means Marx now proposed reflected a pragmatism not entirely consistent with his earlier revolutionary rhetoric. They included organization, mass political action by working-class groups, cooperation between working-class parties of all countries.[12] None of this excluded a revolutionary seizure of power at an historically appropriate moment, but conspicuously absent was any specific reference to revolution in the conspiratorial-Jacobin-Blanquist sense.

Major western European Marxist figures of the pre-First World War period such as Edouard Bernstein, Jean Jaurès, Karl Kautsky, and Rosa Luxemburg, the most apealing of them all, however greatly they differed on a host of subjects, remained in close contact with the original rational humanism of Marx. They sought, as he had, the happiness of *human beings*; socialism was a means to achieve that happiness, not an end in itself. Some, like the Revisionists, Bernstein and Jaures, abandoned revolution altogether, believing that the ultimate triumph of the proletarian cause had become inevitable with the spread of the democratic suffrage and parliamentary institutions. Kautsky retained the revolution as such, but redefined it in a way that left him closer to the Revisionists than is sometimes supposed. A drastic reordering of the class structure was necessary, but that change *could* come about through normal operation of the democratic political process as well as through violence. And Rosa Luxemburg, to whom the victory of the proletariat and the triumph of democracy were synonymous, died in the German revolution at the end of the First World War, a revolution that she unsuccessfully sought to turn into a truly mass popular movement. She was betrayed by authoritarians within as well as without the socialist camp.[13]

The most important exceptions to this development were not western Europeans. Possibly the most catastrophic single result of the War of 1914–18—other than its slaughter—was that it allowed the power, if not the right, to define for most of the world what Marxism meant to pass from the hands of western Europeans into those of the Russian Vladimir Lenin and his successors for at least the next half century. Lenin represents, in part, a logical outgrowth of nineteenth century Marxism, in part a monstrous perversion of it. He was, like Marx, bourgeois, but he viewed humanity and society very differently. If there was anything of the eighteenth century about Lenin it was the Enlightened Despot. Like Frederick the Great or Napoleon he was an elitist, willing to pursue by any means his dream of a classless society in the name of and in the interests, as he defined them, of proletarians and peasants.[14] It made no difference that, so long as there was choice, he had the support of only a small minority of either.[15] Despite the occasional violence of Marx's rhetoric it is difficult to imagine him ordering the death of any man; but Lenin's vision required millions to perish, most of them workers or peasants. Even greater numbers died at the hands of his most notable successor, Josef Stalin. Alexandr Solzhenitsyn has demonstrated that the excesses of the Stalin era were not, as Nikita Khrushchev argued in 1956, aberrations attributable to a tyrant's megalomania; they were integral parts of the system itself.[16] Lenin, in the name of justice, was more than any other person responsible for establishing what has been the twentieth century's most enduring tyranny.

The victory of the Bolsheviks in the Russian Revolution and subsequent civil war enabled Lenin and his successors to arrogate to themselves an infallibility analogous to, but more effective than, that claimed by the Pope. But because most western Marxists refused to recognize that infallible authority to define dogma, Socialism outside the Soviet Union became split down the middle into democratic-humanist and Communist-authoritarian wings. The split has endured to our own day. The prestige of Lenin's version of Marxism was enhanced and its power base made more secure because Germany, in which the more humane and democratic Marxism represented by the Social Democrats came to power at the end of the war in 1918, was the object of hatred and opprobrium to most of the world because of the war-guilt issue. Social-Democratic Germany ceased after a few years to be socialist, and the republic itself succumbed to Hitler's tyranny after a decade and a half of troubled existence.

Although the parallels between the Leninist-Stalinist and the Hitlerian regimes are all too striking, particularly with reference to their destruction of humane values, this is not the place to attempt a balance of the crimes of one against those of the other. The issue of Hitler is relevant here only because it was his coming to power in Germany that made it ultimately impossible for Western Europeans to cope intellectually or otherwise with Stalinism. For noncommunist Marxists the problem was not different from that faced by others committed to the survival of democracy, but it was even more acute. Few West European Socialists viewed with anything but revulsion the stubborn insistence throughout 1932 of the German Communist Party, supported by Stalin and the Comintern, that Social Democrats were the true enemies of the working class: "We cannot and will not abandon our struggle against Social Democracy, for that would be equivalent to abandoning the struggle against the bourgeoisie."[1] Communists even allowed Nazis to join their picket lines during a November 1932 strike against the Berlin Transit Authority.[18] Unlike a few deluded middle-class politicians in Great Britain and France, however, democratic socialists could hardly view Hitler as an acceptable bulwark against the expansion of Stalinist influence in Europe.[19] Since it seemed, and indeed there was little to choose between the two totalitarian systems, middle-class democrats and working-class social democrats both suffered a growing paralysis of will. Throughout the 1930s that paralysis contributed greatly to the impotence displayed by Western democracies.

Among the many examples are the effort of France under Laval's leadership to win Mussolini as an ally in 1935 in order to avoid the intolerable prospect of embracing Stalin, and the acceptance of Chamberlain and Daladier at Munich of the dismemberment of Czechoslovakia because the danger seemed less than in risking war with Hitler in alliance with Stalin.[20] Equally telling was the failure of the Western democracies to provide significant aid to republican Spain during the Spanish Civil War. The Popular Front regime in France, headed by the Socialist Léon Blum and dependent for its parliamentary majority on the bourgeois Radical-Socialists and the Communists as well, found itself incapable of taking meaningful action during the critical early months of the war when the republic might have been saved. Much of the public, including a large part of the Radical-Socialist constituency, feared that any pro-republican policy would involve France in a war on the side of those who, the French Right claimed, had embarked on a "Crusade for Communism." Many noncommunist members of the parliamentary coalition itself were unwilling or afraid to support any policy advocated by their Communist colleagues regardless of its merits.[21] The Conservative government of Stanley Baldwin in Great Britain, which deeply distrusted the Popular Front on both emotional and ideological grounds, made it clear that should France become involved in a continental war arising out of intervention in Spain, she could count on no assistance from London.[22] Blum's later claim that in 1936 he feared a fascist uprising in France itself were the country to become embroiled in Spain on the side of the Loyalists has a certain ex post facto ring.[23] Yet after the ugly riots of February 1934, no premier of the left could wholly ignore that possibility.

The Hitler-Stalin pact, signed a few days before the outbreak of the Second World War, further compounded the confusion of the left in Western Europe. It did, however, shatter to some degree the uncritical support that some noncommunist intellectuals had given the Soviet regime throughout the 1930s.[24] From then until June 22, 1941, when German armies invaded Russia, communist parties in the West followed the lead of the CPSU and denounced the governments of Great Britain and France as "decadent imperialists" because they had taken up arms against Hitler, an action communists attributed to the failure of those powers to accomplish their goal of bringing about a German-Soviet War.[25]

Hitler's invasion of the Soviet Union brought, among other things, a sudden and total reversal of the communist party line throughout the world. The "imperialist war" now became "the common struggle of all peoples" against fascism; revolutionary rhetoric largely disappeared from party organs; in 1943 the Comintern itself was dissolved.[26] The final victory over Germany in 1945, to which the Soviet Union contributed so much blood, not only enhanced that country's power and prestige in world affairs, it gave renewed credence for a time to its assertion of the right to define Marxist dogma. During the war communists had become major elements in the underground resistance in France, the Low Countries, and Italy. In a sense they earned forgiveness for having spread defeatism among the troops on the Western Front during 1939–40.[27] Because of this outstanding resistance record—at least for the rank and file, since most West European communist leaders had spent the war years in Moscow—the party and its ideology emerged from the war with considerably more respectability than either had ever enjoyed in the West before. The new acceptability of communists also benefited from the conviction, widely held at the war's end, that only through some form of socialism could Europe recover and guarantee social justice. Willingness to embrace Marxism, or at least Marxists, and to accept the inevitability of communist participation in postwar governments extended far into the middle class.[28] Those dreams or illusions foundered on the reef of the cold war.

The question of responsibility for the American-Soviet confrontation does not concern us here. What is significant is that the Soviets and their tools, communist parties in other countries, did, in a matter of three years, exhaust the good will that the war had created for them. The Soviet Union denied to the peoples of Eastern Europe freedom not only to choose between Marxism and its capitalistic alternative, but even to decide for themselves between varieties of Marxism. They were obliged and, if necessary, compelled by force to accept communist regimes that served Soviet interests, not those of the local population. It may be that Soviet authorities were truly convinced that working-class interests everywhere coincided with those of the Soviet Union and that their heavy-handed control was not, therefore, properly speaking, imperialistic. It should have surprised no one that Western Europeans, including most Marxists, saw it differently. The continued United States presence troubled many Europeans who feared for their traditional cultural values, but at least the Americans did not employ starvation against the people of a great city as the Soviets did during the Berlin blockade of 1948–49. They did not use tanks to shoot down workers in the streets as both the local communist authorities and the Soviets did during the 1953 East German uprising. Nor did capitalist America use its forces to suppress a revolutionary communist government that clearly enjoyed mass support as the Soviets did in Hungary in 1956 and again in Czechoslovakia as late as 1968. No more could the example of Tito's Yugoslavia be ignored. His Communist Peoples' Democracy served as the splendid example for Soviet propagandists until it categorically refused to allow either its domestic or its foreign policy to be dictated by Moscow. Then it became anathema to the Kremlin.

During the cold war West European Marxism suffered wounds that took a long time to heal. As the euphoria in the West about a socialist future gave way to indignation over the brutal tactics of the Soviets in the East, hostility toward Soviet Communism began also to be directed at the Western communist parties, rightly perceived as its agents. But less justifiably that hostility began to run off on democratic socialists as well. They were caught between two fires: Moscow denounced them as traitors to the working class because they would not slavishly follow its dictates, while the increasingly anticommunist Americans more and more treated them as witting or unwitting tools of the "international Communist conspiracy." In Italy the Communists have since 1948 been effectively excluded from meaningful exercise of power at the national level, although they have controlled an increasing number of municipalities and, with the long-delayed creation of the constitutionally mandated regional governments in 1970, the PCI immediately won control of three of the twenty regions. Socialists, deeply divided internally over the question of cooperation with the Communists or the bourgeois Christian Democrats, have sometimes united into a single party but more frequently have been divided into three. Although the largest, the PSI, was for most of the period since 1962 part of the governing coalition in partnership with the Christian Democrats, Socialists have not, as a minority within the government, been able to claim credit for the few positive achievements but have had to share blame for the failures.[29] It required until 1958 for the Socialists and Communists to be wholly eliminated from power in France, but, with the rise of de Gaulle, eliminated they were, and all efforts to regain their lost position have so far failed despite the "Common Program" adopted by the two parties in 1972 and their impressive showing in the unsuccessful bid for the presidency in 1974.[30] In the Federal Republic of Germany, a special case because of the proximity of the eastern threat, SPD was excluded from participation in national, although not from state, governments until 1969. The Labour Party in Great Britain, socialist but, despite the rhetoric of its radical left wing, only remotely Marxist, governed from 1945 to 1951, but was thereafter out of power for 13 years until 1964.

In another sense, however, West European Leftists were victims of their own success. In every West European country except Italy far-reaching social change *did* take place in the immediate postwar years, those years in which, as in France, moderate socialists and even communists were part of most governments, or, as in Great Britain, where the Labour Party controlled the government completely. Moreover, the *Soziale Marktwirtschaft* devised by Ludwig Erhardt for the Federal Republic was anything but the old capitalism of the nineteenth century. Like Bismarck, Erhardt and Adenauer sought with considerable success to blunt socialist demands by anticipating them. Only in Italy, for a variety of reasons, including poverty and the power of the Church, did the early postwar years pass without a substantial remodeling of the social and economic order. But even Italy became a welfare state on paper. Every Western country, however it described itself, had developed a mixed economy, partly capitalist, partly socialist; only the degree and kind of the mix varied. Of the 10 "unavoidable means of entirely revolutionizing the mode of production" listed in the *Communist Manifesto*,[31] all but two had been achieved to some degree and in some fashion in every advanced West European country by 1950.[32]

The foregoing provides the single most satisfactory explanation of the fact that when revolutionary radicalism reappeared on a significant scale in Western Europe during the early 1960s it bore little resemblance to traditional varieties of Marxism. Youthful revolutionaries of the 1960s who made up what is loosely called the New Left—the term itself is significant—came almost exclusively from the affluent middle class. Some claimed to be Maoist, but their objectives had as little in common with those of Mao Tse-tung as they did with those of Marx, Engels, or Lenin. All these were highly disciplined "organization men," while the antecedents of the new revolutionaries, if any, are the nineteenth-century anarchists Proudhon and Bakunin, or the romantic Jacobin elitist, Auguste Blanqui.[33] The twentieth-century economic order had eliminated for middle-class youth the necessity for unremitting toil. That was something of which their parents sometimes talked, but it had no personal meaning for them. Also gone was the social discipline traditionally produced by fear of unemployment and consequent hunger. The young of postwar Western Europe had grown up under the threat of nuclear annihilation, but, except perhaps as small children, they had no direct personal experience with the consequences of large-scale violence. To these new revolutionaries the concern with class of Marx, Engels, or Lenin was largely irrelevant, even though they appropriated Marxist rhetoric. And Mao's rural communes that they professed to admire had little relevance to industrial Europe. The "enemy" was bureaucracy—any bureaucracy, whether in the form of a private multinational corporation like IBM, a public corporation like the French National Railway, a university, or the state itself. Marx, like the *philosophe* he was, believed implicitly in the dignity of labor and in the liberating potential of education. The revolutionaries of the 1960s had no such feeling for the work ethic and had reacted to their experience with the best that twentieth-century education has to offer by developing a scathing contempt for it and a mindless commitment to its destruction.[34]

In country after country the university became the chief target, in part because it was the most visible servant of the bureaucratic order, and in part because it was by its very nature least able to defend itself. In the United States, France, Italy, the Federal Republic, to mention only the major examples, student disruption often brought the whole process of rational discussion in universities to a halt. Professors and other students became the victims of outright terrorism. Although universities in most West European countries certainly needed reform, the onslaught became so vicious that permanent damage may well have resulted.[35]

On only one occasion did this new anarchist revolutionary wave come close to toppling a major government. This came in the great French upheaval of the spring of 1968.[36] It was also there that the new role of Marxism in Western Europe first became clearly visible.For it was chiefly the refusal of the workers *as a class* to follow the lead of the student radicals that saved de Gaulle's Fifth Republic. Marxism had become part of the establishment. Factory workers, most of them youthful, many of them employed in state-operated enterprises such as Renault, many, probably most, affiliated with communist-controlled unions of the CGT, demanded and ultimately obtained a substantially larger share of the material benefits that had accrued to France during the decade of de Gaulle's rule. That is another way of saying that they did not desire the overthrow of his *system*. They do appear to have hoped fervently that de Gaulle himself could be forced into retirement, and they did sympathize in a general way with student frustration over the rigid absurdities of traditional French education. Together with most other Frenchmen, factory workers were appalled by the brutalities that the riot-control police inflicted upon student demonstrators, and they were willing to exploit ruthlessly the government's impotence to cope with the student uprising for their own economic interests. But they would not join finally in a common effort to overturn the political and social order in alliance with those who put forth slogans such as "Imagination is seizing power," "It is forbidden to forbid," and "Be a realist, ask the impossible."[37]

The leadership of communist-controlled unions and working-class leaders in general appear to have shared the view of their rank and file. The Renault strikers at Boulogne-Billancourt outside Paris refused to admit a delegation of radical students that had marched to the occupied factory to demonstrate solidarity with the workers. The CGT explained that it would not accept "any external interference in the labor movement."[38] Sometime later the communist organ *Humanité* described Jacques Sauvageot, who, together with Daniel Cohn-Bendit and Alain Geismar, came as close to being the leader of the student movement as its anarchic character would tolerate, as "very far from the aspirations and the preoccupations of the world of labor."[39] The student rebellion brought a halt for a time to the entire process of higher education in France. The general strike that followed was the most widespread and effective in history. At its peak 50 percent of the work force was out and economic activity in the country came to a standstill. Yet the two movements remained parallel, never conjoined. The government was able to deal with them separately, and it survived. De Gaulle's surprise decision to appeal to the country by dissolving Parliament and calling for new elections received, after some early confusion, the support of both the Communist Party and the CGT.[40] Those who had flown the red flag would not march under the black flag of anarchism.

Since the capitalist society against which Marx unleashed his thunderbolts has long since ceased to exist, his portrayal of the historical process has lost whatever validity it once had. In advanced industrial countries the working class, much of it organized under Marxist banners, no longer has revolutionary potential. It has rather come to constitute a major reservoir of strength to defend the basic stucture of the existing order wherever that order is subject to democratic control. Thus Marxism appears to have run its course as a revolutionary force in Western Europe. It nonetheless served a profoundly important historical purpose, for it was largely the fears of revolution that it aroused that stimulated the political and economic changes that made revolution no longer an attractive option. Democratic Socialists have now become part of the new political establishment in every West European country, accepted as fully legitimate by everyone except the extremist fringes on the right and left. The Communists, moreover, seem also on the verge of achieving a similar respectability. Having waited, like the early Christians, for the apocalypse that did not come, they have increasingly begun to adjust to reality at whatever cost to doctrinal purity. Georges Marchais, the head of the PCF, speaks of "Communism under French colors," and the personable secretary of the Italian Communist Party, Enrico Berlinguer, urges the *"Compromesso storico"* that will allow Italy to break free of the stagnation of recent years.[41] Both parties are on record as accepting parliamentary government, both have abandoned the "dictatorship of the proletariat," both have stressed their "Europeanism," that is, their independence of the Soviet Union, and both have even given NATO a mild blessing.[42] Moscow too has contributed to this development by espousing detente with the West, thus admitting that the revolution, if not permanently abandoned, has been postponed indefinitely.

The decline of the class struggle as a principle around which to organize political action has been even more dramatic among the democratic socialist parties. When the British Labour Party returned to power in 1964 under the leadership of Harold Wilson, after 13 years in opposition, it had a fundamentally new program. Founded in 1900 primarily to represent the trade union movement, the party was reluctant to acknowledge its debt even to Marx the *philosophe*. It adopted a specifically socialist program only in June of 1918, when it committed itself to "the gradual building up of a new social order" to be marked by "the common ownership of the means of production."[43] Its position was thus hardly different in fact from those that had already been or would shortly be adopted by continental social-democratic parties, proud of their Marxism, but determined to establish a ground that they could defend against the siren song of Bolshevik authoritarianism. Like British Labour they would work to achieve Marx's objectives through democratic, nonrevolutionary means.[44]

Labour's 1945–51 parliamentary majority was the first ever won by a party committed to the total abolition of capitalism. But the long years spent thereafter in opposition took their toll. By 1959 the party was in danger of fragmenting between its militant, rigidly working-class-oriented left wing and its less doctrinaire center, which sought to make converts among the middle class. The largely unexpected defeat in the 1959 election, the third in succession, proved a shock sufficiently great that the moderates under Hugh Gaitskill were able in 1960 to win approval of a redefinition of party objectives, the first since 1918. Henceforth the party would seek only an expansion of public ownership "substantial enough to give the community power over the commanding heights of the economy." It recognized that "both public and private enterprise have a place in the economy."[45] Labour thus gave formal approval to what it had long accepted in practice: an economy partly socialized and partly capitalist, the degree of each to be established by democratic means.

In 1969, five years after Labour's return to office in Great Britain, the SPD for the first time won the right to control the government of the Federal Republic of Germany. Founded in 1875, SPD is the oldest continuously existing social democratic party in the world. It had opted for democracy and gradualism rather than revolution and proletarian dictatorship during the 1918–19 revolution, of which it was the principal instigator. It led a clandestine existence during the Nazi period, and during the first post-Second World War years, under the leadership of Kurt Schumacher, it returned to a much more dogmatic and class-oriented position, partially because it was competing furiously with the Communists for the allegiance of the working class. Three successive national elections made it clear that SPD's continued reference in its programs to the class struggle and to nationalization of basic industries made the party unacceptable to the majority of Germans. It seemed much closer to the Communists than was in fact the case. In 1959, after a long and bitter debate at the Extraordinary Congress held in Bad Godesberg, the party formally renounced the class struggle and common ownership.[46] The Godesberg program declared that "Private ownership of the means of production can claim protection by society as long as it does not hinder the establishment of social justice."[47] In the future the party would stand for "as much competition as possible—as much planning as necessary."[48] It took a decade for the seed planted at Godesberg to bear fruit. SPD became the junior partner in the CDU-SPD grand coalition of 1966, and three years later its leader, Willy Brandt, became Federal Chancellor. Significantly, Brandt's accession came because, after the election of September 23, 1969, the most bourgeois of consequential German parties, the FDP (Free Democrats) chose to enter a coalition headed by Brandt rather than to renew its 20-year alliance with the Christian Democrats.[49] The middle class was now willing to trust SPD with power in a pluralistic parliamentary democracy. Three years later, in the election of November 19, 1972, SPD for the first time in the history of the Federal Republic received more votes than did its perennial rival, CDU—45.9 percent to 44.8 percent—and, although it slipped once more into second position as a result of the October 3, 1976, election, it still commanded the loyalty of FDP and retained control of the government.[50]

In neighboring Austria, small, neutralized, but important because of its geographical position between east and west, 1970 brought a similar development when the Socialist Party (SPÖ) for the first time since the Second World War assumed full responsibility for the government. The 1970 minority regime of Bruno Kreisky achieved full majority status as the result of elections in October 1971 when the Socialists unexpectedly won more than 50 percent of the popular vote and a parliamentary majority of three seats. It retained that majority and control of the government in the elections of October 1975. Unlike the German SPD, SPÖ had participated in coalitions with the more conservative Peoples' Party (ÖVP) from 1945 to 1966. Like it, SPÖ had demonstrated that it could be trusted to defend democracy and tolerate a pluralistic economy. The party had abandoned its doctrinaire Marxist anticlericalism in 1958 and in 1969 repudiated a pledge of support by the Communists (KPÖ).[51]

Only a word need be added about the Scandinavian countries, where Social Democrats have for a half-century enjoyed the advantages conferred by their status as the largest single voting bloc in Denmark, Sweden, and Norway. Scandinavian socialist parties were in their origin Marxist, in fact, offshoots of the German SPD. Because, as neutrals, these countries largely escaped the trauma of the First World War, socialist parties there, unlike those of the rest of Western Europe, continued the orderly movement away from revolutionary ideology toward democratic reformism that had characterized the parties of the Second International, without suffering many of the destructive tensions that rent the movement elsewhere.[52] Ironically, however, Scandinavian social-democratic regimes have come under fire in recent years precisely because they have for so long been part of the political establishment.

They have become victims of the hostility toward *all* governments that has been an increasingly prominent feature of Western politics.[53] Familiarity appears to breed contempt even in the world of democratic socialism. In Sweden the voters recently turned out the Socialists after more than a half-century in favor of those whose policies, however, differ only minimally from those of their predecessors.[54]

Democratic, noncommunist forms of Marxism have then become respectable almost everywhere in the West, and Eurocommunism now appears to be on the threshold of achieving a similar respectability as the left wing of the democratic movement rather than its subverter. The latter development is probably the more important. In the past communism has been chiefly effective as a tool for bringing about rapid industrialization in underindustrialized regions that were not part of traditional Europe—Russia, China, Vietnam, Cuba, and the like—to which Marx's classical revolutionary model had little relevance, rather than in reordering more equitably the distribution of the product in advanced industrial societies. In those countries a communist elite played the historical role that Marx assigned to the bourgeoisie. It seems likely that future successes, if any, of the authoritarian Leninist-Maoist varieties of communism will come in similar countries elsewhere in Asia or in Latin America. It is, however, increasingly probable that Marxism, a basically nineteenth-century ideology, is, in all its forms, as irrelevant to the late twentieth century as the bourgeois capitalist system it denounces.

Marx, Engels, and Lenin, however they may have differed from bourgeois economic theorists like Smith and Mill, shared with them the premise that human ingenuity properly applied and managed would bring about a constant increase in the material standard of living, and that it was at least theoretically possible for society to provide abundance for all. In that sense Marx's dictum, "From each according to his ability, to each according to his needs,"[55] is as succinct a statement of the Enlightenment's optimistic faith in progress as we know. Whether that vision of material comfort for all can be realized in a world plagued by scarcity is open to serious doubt. For the scarcity of the future, unlike that of the past, will be the product not of ignorance or inadequate technology, nor even of the machinations of a selfish ruling class, but of the sheer inadequacy of the planet's resources to sustain its still-growing population. Under those conditions can Marx's vision of a classless society have meaning? Can any society, however structured, meet the goal of "to each according to his needs" in any sense compatible with what Marx meant?

NOTES

1. Karl Marx and Friedrich Engels, *Collected Works*, 7 vols. to date (New York: International Publishers, 1975–77, 6 [Marx and Engels: 1845–48], pp. 481, 519. The final exhortation is all too frequently misquoted as "Working men of *the world*, unite!" The difference is meaningful. The thought of Marx and Engels is more conventional in its acceptance of existing institutions, for example, the nation state, than is often realized.

2. The newest and best study of Marx is David McClellan, *Karl Marx, His Life and Thought* (New York: Harper and Row, 1973).

3. Marx and Engels, *Collected Works*, 6, p. 482.

4. *Capital, A Critique of Political Economy* (New York: Modern Library, 1906), p. 25.

5. See George Lichtheim, *Marxism: An Historical and Critical Study* (New York: Frederick A. Praeger, 1961), pp. 33–40.

6. Marx and Engels, *Collected Works*, 6, pp. 489–90.

7. Reprinted in *The Marx-Engels Reader*, ed. Robert C. Tucker (New York: W. W. Norton and Co., 1971), p. 603. Of the many one-volume anthologies of Marx and Engels, Professor Tucker's is by far the best.

8. Lichtheim, pp. 234–58.

9. Marx and Engels, *Collected Works*, 6, p. 519.

10. Karl Marx, *Selected Works in Two Volumes*, ed. V. Adoratsky (London: Lawrence and Wishart, n.d.), pp. 2, 154–68.

11. *Marx-Engels Reader*, p. 379.

12. Ibid., pp. 379-81.

13. The best general treatment of the history of socialism before the Russian revolution is in appropriate chapters of *Histoire Générale du Socialisme*, ed. Jacques Droz, 2 vols. (Paris: Presses Universitaires de France, 1972–74). On Bernstein, see Peter Gay, *The Dilemma of Democratic Socialism* (New York: Columbia University Press, 1952) and Pierre Angel, *Edouard Bernstein et l'Évolution du Socialisme allemand* (Paris: M. Didier, 1961). On Jaurès, Harvey Goldberg, *The Life of Jean Jaurès* (Madison: University of Wisconsin Press, 1962). There seems to be no modern study of Kautsky. For Rosa Luxemburg, see J. P. Nettl, *Rosa Luxemburg*, 2 vols. (London: Oxford University Press, 1966).

14. See, for example, V. I. Lenin, "What Is To Be Done?" in *Selected Works*, 3 vols. (Moscow and New York: International Publishers, 1967), pp. 1, 97–256, esp. 189–202.

15. The Bolsheviks, despite their arrogant appropriation of a name derived from the adjective for "more," remained, until other parties and factions were forcibly suppressed, a minority even among Russian Marxists. Cf. Lenin to G. F. Fyodorov, Aug. 9, 1918: "It is obvious that a whiteguard insurrection is being prepared in Nizhni. . . . organize *immediately* mass terror, *shoot and deport the hundreds* of prostitutes (italics in the original) who are making drunkards of the soldiers, former officers and the like. . . . You must act with all energy. Mass searches. Execution for concealing arms. Mass deportation of Mensheviks and unreliables." V. I. Lenin, *Collected Works*, Vol. 35 [Letters, February, 1912–December, 1922] (Moscow: Progress Publishers, 1966), p. 349. See also Alexander I. Solzhenitsyn, *The Gulag Archipelago*, 1918–1956, tr. Thomas P. Whitney (New York: Harper and Row, 1973), pp. 27–37.

16. Solzhenitsyn, esp. pp. 298–373. See also George H. Leggett, "Lenin, Terror, and Political Policy," *Survey*, 21 (Autumn, 1975): 157–87.

17. Wilhelm Florin, Communist member of the German Reichstag, quoted by Siegfried Bahne, "Die kommunistische Partei Deutschlands," in *Das Ende der Parteien, 1933*, ed. Erich Matthias and Rudolf Morsey [Veroffentlichungen der Kommission fur Geschichte des Parliamentarismus und der politischen Parteien] (Düsseldorf: Droste Verlag, 1960), p. 676.

18. Ibid., p. 680.

19. See, for example, Margaret George, *The Warped Vision: British Foreign Policy, 1933–1939* (Pittsburgh: University of Pittsburgh Press, 1965), pp. 126–37.

20. The often-repeated charge that Chamberlain and Daladier deliberately sacrificed Czechoslovakia in order to divert Hitler eastward and thereby promote a German-Soviet war cannot be proved or disproved. See D. F. Fleming, *The Cold War and Its Origins, 1917-1960*, 2 vols. (Garden City, N.Y.: Doubleday, 1961), 1, pp. 84–87, and Gaetano Salvemini, *Prelude to World War II* (Garden City, N.Y.: Doubleday, 1954), pp. 10–11. What is certain is that Chamberlain felt "the most profound distrust of Russia." See Keith Feiling, *The Life of Neville Chamberlain* (London: Macmillan and Co., 1946), p. 403. In a letter to his sister written early in 1938 he accused the Russians of "stealthily and cunningly pulling all the strings behind the scenes to get us involved in war with Germany." (Ibid., p. 347.) On March 18, 1939, Chamberlain admitted that up until the German invasion of Bohemia on March 15, British policy had been based "on the assumption that Britain could get on 'better terms with the Dictator Powers.'"—Robert Manne, "The British Decision of Alliance with Russia, May, 1939," *Journal of Contemporary History*, 9 (1974): 7. As late as May 20 he was quoted as still preferring to resign rather than sign an alliance with the Soviets. Ibid., p. 25.

21. George G. Windell, "Leon Blum and the Crisis over Spain, 1936," *The Historian*, 24 (1962): 423–49.

22. Ibid., pp. 428; 430, note 18; 446–47; and 446, note 68.

23. Ibid., pp. 437; 446–48; and 447, note 69.

24. The *Union des Intellectuels Francais* published on August 29, 1939, a manifesto that expressed "stupefaction in face of this turnabout." It was signed by, among others, Frédéric and Irène Joliot-Curie.—A. Rossi, *Les Communistes Francais pendant la drôle de guerre: une page d'histoire* (Paris: Iles d'or, 1951), p. 31.

25. See Julius Braunthal, *History of the International*, tr. John Clark, 2 vols. (New York and Washington: Frederick A. Praeger, 1967), 2, pp. 504–25; and "Extracts from an article by [George] Dimitrov on the tasks of the working class in the War," reprinted in *The Communist International, 1919–1943: Documents*, ed. Jane Degras, 3 vols. (London and New York: Oxford University Press, 1956–65), 3, pp. 448–59.

26. Braunthal, 2, pp. 254–58.

27. Ibid., pp. 527–30; Jacques Fauvet and Alain Duhamel, *Histoire du Parti Communiste Francais*, 2 vols. (Paris: Fayard, 1964–65), 2, pp. 86–135. On Communist efforts to undermine French morale during the "phony war," see Rossi, *Communistes Francais . . .*, which reproduces photographically numerous examples of their underground publications.

28. See for example, Jacques Chapsal, *La Vie politique en France depuis 1940* (Paris: Presses Universitaires de France, 1966), ch. IV, esp. pp. 112–19; and Guiseppe Mammarella, *Italy After Fascism: A Political History, 1943–1965* (Notre Dame, Ind.: University of Notre Dame, 1966), pp. 17–95.

29. John Earle, *Italy in the 1970's* (London: David and Charles, 1975), pp. 50–55, 87–89, 198–99.

30. For the first time the PCF formally accepted *"l'alternance au pouvoir,"* that is, the obligation to resign in response to an adverse vote. See *L'Année Politique, Économique, Sociale et Diplomatique en France, 1972*, ed. Edouard Bonnefous et al. (Paris: Presses Universitaires de France, 1973), pp. 48–49.

31. Marx and Engels, *Collected Works*, 6, p. 505.

32. Abolition of private property in land and equal liability of all to labor.

33. For Proudhon, see Robert L. Hoffman, *Revolutionary Justice: The Social and Political Theory of P. J. Proudhon* (Urbana, Ill.: University of Illinois Press, 1972). For Bakunin, see E. H. Carr, *Michael Bakunin* (New York: Macmillan Co., 1937), and for Blanqui see Droz, 1, pp. 395–96 and Paul Louis, *Cent cinquante Ans de Pensée socialiste* (Paris: M. Rivière, 1947), pp. 65–73.

34. The literature on student uprisings of the 1960s and early 1970s is already enormous and can only be sampled here. Works such as *Politics of the New Left*, ed. Mathew Stolz (Beverly Hills, Calif.: Glencoe Press, 1971), and *The Radical Left: the Abuse of Discontent*, ed. William P. Gerberding and Duane E. Smith (Boston: Houghton Mifflin Co., 1970) present collections of essays by various authors, those in the first mostly favorable, those in the the second mildly unfavorable to the rebels. The best treatments are found in periodicals. See for example, "Rebellion der Jugend: Dokumentation einer Fernsehsendung," *Frankfurter Hefte: Zeitschrift fur Kultur und Politik*, 23 (July 1968): 453–78; Alexander Schwann, "Macht Demokratisierung die Universitat unregierbar?" ibid., 25 (April 1970): 259–67, and the Sonderheft, devoted entirely to "Bildung," of the same journal, 26 (April 1971). See also Oreste Scalzone, "Sur l'occupation de la faculté des lettres à l'université de Rome," *Les Temps Modernes*, 23 (May–June 1968): 1996–2001; Russell Stetler, "Les revolutionnaires impatients," ibid., 25 (June–July 1969): 2130–150; Jean-Marcel Bouguereau, "Le mouvement des étudiants berlinois: un précédent?" ibid., 24 (July 1968): 1–69; Lawrence Stone, "Two Cheers for the University," *New York Review of Books*, 11 (Aug. 22, 1968): 21–22; Stephen Spender, "The Young in Berlin," ibid., 11 (Sept. 12, 1968): 37–40; and F. W. Dupee, "The Uprising at Columbia," ibid., 11 (Sept. 26, 1968): 20–38.

35. See for example, David Schoenbaum, "The Free University of Berlin, or, How Free Can a University Be?" *AAUP Bulletin*, 59 (March 1973): 5–9; Henry L. Mason, "Reflections on the Politicized University, I. The Academic Crisis in the Federal Republic of Germany," ibid., 60 (Sept. 1974): 299–310; "II. Triparity and Tripolarity in the Netherlands," ibid., 60 (Dec. 1974): 383–400.

36. For a sympathetic general treatment see Daniel Singer, *Prelude to Revolution: France in May, 1968* (New York: Hill and Wang, 1970). Alain Schnapp and Pierre Vidal-Naquet, *The French Student Uprising, November, 1967–June, 1968: An Analytical Record*, tr. Maria Jolas (Boston: Beacon Press, 1971), reproduces much of the ephemeral student political writing of the period as well as attempting an interpretation. See also appropriate sections of *L'Année politique . . . 1968* (Paris:Presses Universitaires de France, 1969), and Lucio Magri, "Reflexions sur les événements de Mai," *Les Temps Modernes*, 25 (Aug.–Sept. 1969): 1–45, 25 (Oct. 1969): 455–92, and 25 (Nov. 1969): 684–728; Michel Johan, La C.G.T. et le mouvement de Mai," ibid., 24 (Aug.–Sept. 1968): 327–75; Stephen Spender, "Paris in the Spring," *New York Review of Books*, 11 (July 11, 1968): 18–26; and E.J. Hobsbawm, "Birthday Party," ibid., 12 (May 22, 1969): 4–12.

37. Nowhere is the anarchic (and perhaps anarchist) character of the student revolt more apparent than in the marvelous graffiti that it produced. The quotations are from an excellent collection of them, Julien Besançon, *Les Murs ont la Parole: Journal mural, Mai, 68* (Paris: Claude Tchou, 1968), pp. 42, 89, 146–47. Other examples that reveal the gap between students and workers are "The unions are whorehouses," ibid., p. 68; "Humanity will be happy only when the last capitalist is hanged by the intestines of the last Leftist," ibid., p. 158; and, most pointed of all, "I am a Marxist, leaning toward Groucho," ibid., p. 87.

38. *L'Année politique . . . 1968*, p. 39.

39. Ibid., p. 46. *Humanité* charged that Cohn-Bendit "was playing the game of M. Pompidou," Ibid., p. 39. A worker (member of a CGT union) was quoted as saying, "Cohn-Bendit is an agent of the CIA and of Pompidou. It is the government that wanted all this." Another, however, declared, "I would like to carry flowers to Cohn-Bendit because without him we would not have gotten anything." Gavi, *Les Temps Modernes*, 24 (July 1968): 90–91.

40. Mme. Vaillant-Coutourier, one of the best known PCF figures, said during the election campaign, "We act within the limits of legality." The director of *Humanité* wrote at about the same time, "The Communist Party does not lay claim to power. It does not even seek to control the direction of the government." *L'Année politique . . . 1968*, p. 50.

41. Georges Marchais, the secretary-general of the party, used the phrase in his keynote

address to the 22nd party congress in Paris on Feb. 4, 1976. New York *Times*, Feb. 6, 1976, p. 1. See also Heinz Timmerman, "Frankreichs Kommunisten: Wandel durch Mitarbeit," *Europa Archiv*, 28 (May 10, 1973): 300–10, and Jean Kanapa, "A 'New Policy' of the Communists?" *Foreign Affairs*, 55 (Jan. 1977): 280–94. Kanapa is head of the Foreign Affairs Section of the PCF politbureau. On Italy see Sergio Segre, "The 'Communist Question' in Italy," *Foreign Affairs*, 54 (July 1976): 691–707, and Arrigo Levi, "Berlinguer's Communism: An Interview and an Appraisal," *Survey*, 18 (Summer 1972): 1–15. Segre is head of the International Department of the PCI.

42. In November 1975, the two parties signed a common charter that endorsed Communist participation in a multiparty political system. It specifically condemned the one-party rule of the USSR. New York *Times*, Feb. 5, 1976, p. 3. See also Kanapa, *Foreign Affairs*, 55: 291; Segre, ibid., 54: 699–702; and Wilfried Loth, "Sozialisten und Kommunisten in Frankreich: Zwischenbilanz einer Strategie," *Europa Archiv*, 30 (Jan. 25, 1975): 39–58.

43. G.D.H. Cole, *A History of the Labour Party from 1914* (London: Routledge and K. Paul, 1948), pp. 53–56. The Resolutions of the Party Conference of June 1918 are summarized by Cole, pp. 65–71, and the Party Constitution of that year is reproduced verbatim, pp. 71–81.

44. The best general treatment of this development is G.D.H. Cole, *A History of Socialist Thought*, 5 vols (New York: St. Martin's Press, 1959–65), vol. IV, parts 1 and 2, *Communism and Social Democracy, 1914–1931*. The work covers a great deal more than its excessively modest title suggests. See also, Droz, *Socialisme democratique*, chs. 9–12.

45. Harold Wilson, "Wilson Defines British Socialism," New York *Times Magazine*, Sept. 15, 1963, p. 32. See also Ralph Miliband, *Parliamentary Socialism: A Study of the Politics of Labour*, 2nd ed. (London: Merlin Press, 1972), pp. 344–47; and *Toward Socialism*, ed. Perry Anderson and Robin Blackburn (Ithaca, N.Y.: Cornell University Press, 1966).

46. See Douglas A. Chalmers, *The Social Democratic Party of Germany: From Working Class Movement to Modern Political Party* (New Haven: Yale University Press, 1964); David Childs, *From Schumacher to Brandt: The Story of German Socialism, 1945–1965* (Oxford: Pergamon Press, 1966); Harold Kent Schellenger, *The S.P.D. in the Bonn Republic: A Socialist Party Modernizes* (The Hague: Martinus Nijhoff, 1968), pp. 57–110, and Theo Pirker, *Die SPD nach Hitler: Die Geschichte der Sozial-demokratischen Partei Deutschlands, 1945–1964* (Munich: Rütten and Loening, 1965), pp. 275–85. Pirker, p. 285, says, "The SPD ceased in a programmatic sense to be an anti-capitalist, socialist, or radical-democratic party with the adoption of the Godesberg Program." The judgment seems excessively harsh.

47. *Basic Programme of the Social Democratic Party of Germany* (Bonn: Social Democratic Party of Germany, n.d.), p. 11.

48. Ibid., p. 10. On the new direction of SPD see also, Erich Ollenhauer, "Zum Godesberger Grundsatzprogramm," in his *Reden und Aufsätze*, ed. Fritz Sänger (Hannover: J.H.W. Dietz, Nachs, 1964), pp. 275–306.

49. New York *Times*, Sept. 29, 1969, p. 1; Oct. 1, pp. 1, 12; Oct. 2, p. 1; Oct. 4, pp. 1, 2. The FDP share of the vote declined from 9.5% in 1965 to 5.8% in 1969.

50. Ibid., Nov. 20, 1972, p. 1; Oct. 4, 1976, pp. 1, 6.

51. The best brief treatment of Austrian history since World War I in English is Elisabeth Barker, *Austria, 1918–1972* (Coral Gables, Fla.: University of Miami Press, 1973). See esp. pp. 254–64.

52. Droz, pp. 270–83. See also J.A. Lauwerys, *Scandinavian Democracy* (Copenhagen: American Scandinavian Foundation, 1958); Walter Galenson, *Labor in Norway* (New York: Russell and Russell, 1970); W. Glyn Jones, *Denmark* (New York: Frederick A. Praeger,

1970), pp. 182–218; Stewart Oakley, *A Short History of Sweden* (New York: Frederick A. Praeger, 1966), pp. 229–56; and Olaf Ruin, "Patterns of Government Composition in Multi-Party Systems: The Case of Sweden," *Scandinavian Political Studies*, 4 (1969): 71–87.

53. Bo Särlvik, "Voting Behavior in Shifting 'Election Winds': An Overview of the Swedish Elections, 1964–1968," *Scandinavian Political Studies* 5 (1970): 241–83; Stein Rokken and Henry Valen, "The Election to the Norwegian Storting in September, 1969," ibid., 287–99; Harry Forsell, "The Elections in Sweden in September, 1970: Politics in a Multi-Level Election," ibid., 6 (1971): 201–11; Ole Borre, "The General Election in Denmark, January, 1975: Toward a New Structure of the Party System," ibid., 10 (1975): 211–16; Hans Jorgen Nielsen, "The Uncivic Culture: Attitudes towards the Political System in Denmark and the Vote for the Progress Party, 1973–1975," ibid., 11 (1976): 147–55; Steen Sauerberg, "The Uncivic Culture: Communication and the Political System in Denmark, 1973–1975," ibid., pp. 157–63.

54. New York *Times*, Sept. 20, 1976, p. 1; Sept. 21, p. 1; Sept. 23, p. 2; Sept. 24, I, p. 12.

55. "Critique of the Gotha Program," reprinted in *Marx-Engels Reader*, p. 388.

CHAPTER

10

SOCIALIST TRANSNATIONAL COOPERATION AND THE FUTURE

Werner J. Feld

The essays presented in this volume confirm that the West European socialist parties do not constitute a homogeneous system. Marked differences in ideological pursuit and political strategies distinguish not only the parties in the northern, middle, and southern tiers, but there is also no consistent uniformity within the tiers. Nevertheless, instruments for multilateral cooperation exist: they are 1) the Second Socialist International, 2) the Confederation of Social Democratic Parties of the European Community, and 3) the Socialist Party Group in the European Parliament, reinforced by contacts with socialist members of the assemblies of the Council of Europe and the West European Union.

THE SOCIALIST INTERNATIONAL

The Socialist International was founded in 1889 on the 100th anniversary of the storming of the Bastille in Paris. It was the successor of the International Workers Association that was set up by English and French labor leaders in 1864. The International was (and remains) a protest movement against the capitalist system and against the "exploitation of human beings by human beings." It advocated the solidarity of workers in all countries of the world.

After World War II the International was revived in 1951 during a meeting of the Committee of the International Socialist Conference (OMISCO) in Frankfurt. Socialist parties from 30 countries participated in this conference and agreed on a basic declaration according to which democratic socialism must not only overcome the capitalist system, but also must sharply distinguish itself from communism with its rigid dogmatism and heavy-handed communist party dictatorship. For the Frankfurt conferees, despite differences in ideological concepts and in sociocultural as well as econopolitical conditions in their respective countries, the common goal was "a society with social justice, higher welfare, freedom, and world peace."[1]

The significance of the Frankfurt conference has been the reestablishment of the Socialist International after World War II in its function as an organizational liaison instrument. The International is composed of 54 socialist parties in all parts of the world with nearly 14 million individual members. Since its origin was in Europe, it is not surprising that the socialist parties of Western Europe have a dominant position. The International's presidents and vice presidents have always been Europeans and its administrative seat is in London.

For the coordindation of political concepts and actions the International has four organs: The Congress, The General Council, The Executive Committee, and the Secretariat. The Executive Committee has become de facto the most important organ largely because it is composed of the secretaries general of the parties and of many prominent party experts on foreign policy. It meets, on the average, every two months and discusses current political problems. Although coordination of concepts and actions is attempted, perhaps more in the Executive Comittee than in the other organs, its decisions are not binding on individual parties and therefore common policies are very rarely adopted. This is especially the case in the field of foreign policy where national circumstances and interests place severe constraints on those socialist parties that are in charge of their governments, but have also to be carefully considered by the parties that are in the opposition in their respective countries.

During meetings of the Congresses and the General Council, no effort is ever made to design concrete policies or to prepare political decisions. The significance of these bodies lies in the fact that they offer opportunities for leading personalities of the individual parties, often party chiefs or prime ministers, to get together for discussion and the exchange of information. For example, during the Congress of 1966 in Stockholm, Pietro Nenni, then leader of the PSI, explained the relations of its party to the Communists. Other themes at later Congresses were the *Ostpolitik* of the Federal Republic, the expansion of the European Communities, and the Helsinki Conference on European Security. Sometimes resolutions are passed regarding particular world problems such as development aid to the Third World and pollution.[2] But no new foreign policy initiatives are undertaken by the Congresses and their main function, as well as those of the other bodies of the International, remains to serve as an important communications and liaison mechanism.

THE FEDERATION OF SOCIALIST PARTIES OF THE EC

In 1974 the Federation of Socialist Parties was created as the culmination of a long process to make cooperation among the EC socialist parties more effective. This process began in 1957 when the six socialist parties represented in Common Assembly of the European Coal and Steel Community set up a Liaison Office composed of one representative of each party. Its initial function was to meet regularly to deal with current issues and to convene every two years a Congress of the Socialist Parties. The Liaison Office was also to work closely with the Socialist Party Group in the Assembly, later the European Parliament, and this organizational arrangement was basically maintained until the Federation took over its functions in 1974.

The Congresses were held sometimes more often than biennially, but between 1966 and 1971 they did not convene at all. The 1962 Congress in Paris adopted a "Common Program for Action by the Social Democratic Parties of the EC"; however, the severe EC crisis in 1965, when France refused to participate in institutional proceedings, dampened the enthusiasm for integration on the part of the socialist parties and new efforts for closer institutionalized cooperation were not made until the 1971 Congress in Brussels. With the expansion of the Community, the Irish and Danish parties were drawn into the cooperation efforts during the Congress of 1973 in Bonn, but British Labour Party representation materialized only later.

The Liaison Office, often referred to as the "Bureau," assumed an increasingly important role in strengthening the relations and contacts among the parties. A representative of the Socialist International has been a permanent fixture of the office, and at times observers of socialist parties outside the Community were invited to the general meetings held by the Liaison Office, which take place at least four times a year. Leading members of the Socialist Party Group in the European Parliament and the Council of Europe have also participated.[3]

Perhaps the most significant means of cooperation among the socialist parties of the EC have been the Congresses, as is also reflected in some of the studies in this volume. Leading party personalities regularly attend and debate the issues, with much space given to the proceedings in the news media. Resolutions adopted at these Congresses have provided policy outlines for the integration of Europe, the democratization of the Community, the harmonization of the national laws and economic policies of member states, and other matters affecting the development of the Community. Other foreign policy issues such as the Nuclear Nonproliferation Treaty and relations with the East European countries have also been discussed. However, it must be stressed that none of the resolutions passed is binding on the national parties. Indeed, in view of the differences in philosophical orientations, political programs, and goals pursued by individual parties, the Congresses occasionally have become food for intensive debates, with consensus often being quite elusive. Although proposals have been made to give decisions adopted unanimously by the Liaison Office and receiving a two-thirds majority by the delegates of a Congress compulsory force, it is doubtful that such proposals will find acceptance unless watered down considerably. The reason is that the national interests and operational conditions of the parties do not coincide. As a consequence, the creation of a European socialist party to become active parallel with the national parties, which has been advocated by European enthusiasts among the party members, has little chance of realization. It would undoubtedly entail a loss of power and prestige for the national party elites[4] and would place major constraints on the decisional latitudes of the national parties, impeding the full utilization of their political power within the national political systems. These considerations may apply less to the smaller member states, such as the Benelux countries, which, in the exercise of their economic and political autonomy, depend more on external circumstances than, for example, West Germany or France and therefore might be less reluctant to subject themselves to common Community-wide regulations. In fact, it may well be the differences in objective interests and perceptions of the European system's external environment between the larger and the small member states that lie at the heart of the Community's integration problems.[5]

THE SOCIALIST PARTY GROUP IN THE EUROPEAN PARLIAMENT

The final instrument of interparty cooperation among the socialist parties is the Party Group in the EP. It is the second largest group, trailing only the Christian Democrats. It is led by an Executive Committee that has political steering and coordination functions as well as administrative responsibilities.

In the party group sessions any matter may be discussed and an attempt is made to reach common positions. Votes are taken, but they are not binding on individual parliamentarians; their purpose is to determine how much consensus can be attained on certain issues and to identify national or ideological conflicts before they become apparent on the floor of the EP.

Since the European Parliament has very limited powers and no legislative functions, and therefore the national political consequences of voting behavior are generally minimal, it has not been difficult for the socialists in the EP to present a fairly cohesive image. In fact, the cohesion factor of the Socialist Party Group in the EP has been higher than that of other groupings.[6]

The significance of the Socialist Party Group as a means of interparty cooperation is diminished by the fact that multilateral contacts between it and parliamentary groupings in the national legislatures rarely occur. Most contacts and interactions are limited to relations and communications between the national delegations to the EP and their parties in the home parliament, and the effectiveness of these channels frequently is impaired by the low prestige that many European parliamentarians have in the eyes of their national colleagues.[7]

In sum, then, the current limited importance and peripheral position of the EP in the EC institutional framework facilitates the achievement of consensus within the Socialist Party Group. It is in its political interest to support the EP as a possible motor for integration progress, and therefore the Group members act as an interest group since integration progress may mean to them greater power and perhaps higher esteem in their countries. But this factor does not reduce the substantial differences among the national socialist parties and should not lead to the conclusion that the Socialist Party Group in the EP is a very effective instrument for interparty cooperation. Whether and how this will be altered when direct EP elections are instituted is difficult to predict, but considerable doubts persist that important changes will occur unless the Parliament is given expanded powers, an unlikely prospect at present.[8]

INFLUENTIAL VARIABLES FOR SOCIALIST PARTY POLICY FORMATION

From the nine studies several variables can be identified that appear to be influential in the formulation of the foreign policy positions adopted by the individual parties. They are:

1. *The strength of the nationalist communist party and its relationship to the socialists.* The degree of CP independence from Moscow may also have a bearing.

The great power of the CP in Italy, France, and Portugal cannot be disregarded when the socialist party leadership in these countries seeks to evolve foreign policy positions, as their nature may affect future electoral outcomes. The surprising comeback in the communist vote during the municipal elections in Portugal in December 1976 (from 8 to 18 percent of total votes cast) illustrates the continuing political challenge to the SP in that country. When a "common program" exists between the SP and CP, as in France, the relationship between the two parties has important implications for the foreign policy stand that the SP may adopt. Somewhat divergent positions by the SP could well be useful at times to make that party more attractive to the voters. In an interview given to syndicated columnist Joseph Kraft in May of 1977, Mitterand stressed the need to demonstrate his and the PS's independence on occasion, and thereby maintain the Socialists as the lead partner in the coalition.[9] Recent trends in France suggest a strengthening of the Socialist Party vis-a-vis the Communists although the cases for this trend may flow from the respective foreign policy positions only to a very minor extent. Nevertheless, it is interesting that the French Communist Party has, as already noted in the Introduction, abandoned its opposition to France's membership in NATO and in fact supports it now.

For the British and German socialist parties, foreign policy concern about the electoral strategies of the indigenous communist parties can be negligible, as the former have been traditionally strong bulwarks against the spread of communism. The SPD continues its strong stand against any kind of cooperation with the Communists and condemns any deviation from this policy, as can be seen by the disciplinary proceedings against the elected head of the JUSOs (Young Socialists), Klaus-Une Benneter, for violation of this principle.[10]

Norway and Sweden seem to constitute an "in-between" category of countries in which strong socialist parties do face competition from communist parties and other leftist party groupings (Norway) for the allegiance and vote especially of the working population. However, the influence of this competition on foreign policy attitudes of the two Scandinavian parties appears to be relatively minor.

2. *The degree of ideological commitment.* This commitment to various shades of Marxism colors perceptions of the international arena and thereby is likely to shape foreign policy attitudes in the socialist parties. It is perhaps lowest in the SPD although the JUSOs continually clamor for the greater ideological fervor. During the last few years, ideological commitment seems to have been quite high in the French PS, as Huntzinger's study suggests, and this may have been partly responsible for the remarkable recovery of the French socialists. The Scandinavian socialist parties may again be intermediate cases, with strong inclinations toward pragmatism. The ideological commitment of the Italian SP may be more rhetoric than substance, and in Portugal the period of "pluralism" has been too short to form a firm judgment and may be influenced by the competing concepts of Eurocommunism.

3. *Internal factionalism.* As our studies suggest, factionalism, a normal feature in most democratic parties, by its very nature impedes the environment of clear-cut foreign policy positions. It is compounded by

different degrees and shades of ideological commitment that prevail in individual partv organizations.

4. *Links to NGOs (nongovernmental organizations), mainly labor unions*. The links of socialist parties with labor unions are especially strong in Great Britain and West Germany, where they had significant, although different, effects on governmental policies toward the EC, and to a lesser degree on NATO and detente policy stands. Labor union links with the socialist parties in France, Italy, and Portugal are considerably weaker and their impact on foreign policy positions of these parties seems to be minor.

5. *The national economic environment*, finally, plays a role in the foreign policy stands of the socialist parties. Poor economic conditions in a particular country are likely to place constraints on the development of these positions and on the intensity of their pursuit. Great Britain and Portugal are cases in point, although financial aid seems to us the way to Britain through a large IMF loan, and to Portugal through the European Community and the United States.

PROJECTIONS FOR THE FUTURE

With circumstances varying widely from socialist party to socialist party in different countries, specifics of their foreign policy positions and particular emphases are apt to be far from uniform. Adding to the disparity in individual positions is the fact that some parties control or participate in the government of their countries, while others are in the opposition. In case of the latter, the foreign policy positions might be less conservative, tend to be more ideology-oriented, and accept greater risks. Variations can also be seen between the parties of Northern and Central Europe on the one hand and the Southwest part of the continent on the other, which clearly emerge from our studies. Nevertheless, these studies also suggest some broad similarities:

1. There is broad support for progress in the European Community development toward a more politically integrated unit provided that "democratization" can be enhanced and the emerging system gradually conforms to social-democratic goals and the tenets of Eurosocialism. How deep is this support cannot be ascertained with accuracy. Indeed, it may be shallow. The activities of the Confederation of Social Democratic Parties since its establishment in 1974 seem to involve more rhetoric than actual coordination of individual party programs, a factor that may be essential for success in the planned direct elections to the European Parliament.

2. All parties discussed recognize the need for the continuation of NATO, but some, such as the SPD, give it more enthusiastic support than others, for example the French PS, which may be partly due to the influence of the intellectually powerful CERES organization and the Common Program with the Communists, although the latter have now also recognized the need for France to remain party to the NATO Treaty. It is noteworthy that the Spanish leader of the Socialists, Felipe Gonzalez, has expressed himself against entry of his country into NATO and against all foreign military bases in Spain.[11] But whether Gonzalez can persist in this stand after the new Spanish government has been installed is far from certain. Of course, the Swedish attitude is affected by the traditional neutrality policy. Moreover, the high cost of a strong Swedish defense system is deplored by some Swedish Social Democrats.

3. The relations with Communist East Europe are influenced by geography—note the Federal Republic's exposed location—and ideology. There appears to be broad support for the continuation of detente policies, including cultural, scientific, and technological exchange and trade, which support, however, now shows somewhat of a downward trend. The emphasis on human rights is likely to approved but not without some concern for the conseuqnces. The negotiations for the mutual reduction of conventional forces, stalled at present, will be supported, but the long-range goal of some socialist parties, especially the French but also left-wing factions in others, is the simultaneous dissolution of both NATO and the Warsaw Pact.[12] This might lead to a truly independent and democratic socialist Europe, the cherished objective of the majority of socialists in Western Europe; and to this end the PS in France might want to continue the current policy of maintaining and perhaps expanding the nuclear *force de frappe* if it were to assume a major role in the French government after the 1978 elections.

4. Atlantic economic interdependence is generally considered as beneficial, although the use of Atlantic relations for intervention into the domestic politics of European countries is frowned upon in most socialist circles.

In a nutshell, then, the Atlantic relationship as symbolized by NATO and transatlantic economic interdependence remains in principle the anchor of safety for the West European socialist parties examined, with Sweden, of course, an exception in respect to NATO. The European Community system is accepted as useful, but ideological considerations tend to color the parties' support. With the strategic and economic bases thus perceived as being covered, detente policies toward Eastern Europe may be pursued with some vigor, policies to which no alternative is perceived.

NOTES

1. Norber Gresch, "Die Zusammenarbeit der Partien des demokratischen Sozialismus in Westeuropa," in *Europaische Schriften*, vol. 42/43 (Bonn: Institute Europaische Politik, 1976), p. 156.

2. Ibid., p. 173.

3. Ibid., p. 198.

4. See Werner J. Feld and John K. Wildgen, *Domestic Political Realities and European Unification* (Boulder, Colo.: Westview Press, 1976), pp. 92–119, 152–171.

5. For more details, ibid., pp. 7–89.

6. Gresch, op. cit., p. 189.

7. Some of the EP members are political "have-beens" or individuals whose prospects for climbing the national political ladder of success were doubtful. See Feld and Wildgen, op. cit., pp. 110–19.

8. Ibid.

9. *International Herald-Tribune*, May 20, 1977, p. 6. However, in his TV debate earlier in May 1977 with Prime Minister Raymond Barre, Communist cost figures for the implementation of the Common Program that were released shortly before the debate seem to have embarrassed Mitterand and revealed some of the vulnerabilities of the coalition. (See *International Herald-Tribune*, May 14–15, 1977.)

10. *Der Spiegel* (vol. 31, no. 21, May 16, 1977), pp. 70–80.

11. *Der Tagesspiegel* (Berlin), May 10, 1977, p. 6.

12. This may also be the objective of the JUSOs in Germany while the present leadership and mainstream of the SPD remains a staunch supporter of NATO's continuation.

ABOUT THE EDITOR AND CONTRIBUTORS

WERNER J. FELD is a Professor of Political Science at the University of New Orleans. He is the author of numerous publications, including *Transnational Business Collaboration Among Common Market Countries* (1970), *Nongovernmental Forces and World Politics* (1972), *The European Community in World Affairs* (1976), and *Domestic Political Realities and European Unification* (with John K. Wildgen) (1976). In addition, Dr. Feld is the author of more than 50 articles in various journals. He received a law degree from the University of Berlin and a Ph.D. in political science from Tulane University.

NILS ANDRÉN is head of the Division for International and Social Studies at the National Defence Research Institute in Stockholm, Sweden. Dr. Andrén has published in Swedish and comparative government and in international and strategic studies. He was Professor of Political Science in Copenhagen, Denmark, 1967–69 and previously held various university positions in Sweden. Dr. Andrén holds a Fil. Dr. (Ph.D.) from the University of Uppsala, Sweden.

FULVIO ATTINA teaches International Relations at the Political Science Department of the University of Florence. He is author of *I conflitti internazionali, Analisi e Misurazione* (1976) and coauthor of a number of articles on different subjects: arms control, parliamentary committees on foreign affairs, peace research, and events analysis. He is a member of the Editorial Advisory Board of *International Interactions*.

THOMAS C. BRUNEAU is Associate Professor of Political Science at McGill University, Montreal. He has published widely on topics dealing with Brazil and Portugal. On Brazil, he has published *The Political Transformation of the Brazilian Catholic Church* (London: Cambridge University Press, 1974), also in Portuguese; his articles also appear in several journals, including the *Latin American Research Review* and *Journal of Interamerican Studies and World Affairs*. On Portugal, he has coauthored a book with Paulino Gomes, *Eanes: Porque o Poder?* (Lisbon: Intervoz, 1976) and published more than a half dozen articles in North America, Europe, and Australia. Professor Bruneau received his M.A. and Ph.D. degrees in political science from the University of California at Berkeley.

CHARLES R. FOSTER is executive secretary of the Committee on Atlantic Studies and secretary-treasurer of the Conference Group on German Politics, an independent organization of scholars devoted to the study of German affairs. He has previously been on the faculties of Indiana University, College of William and Mary, and DePauw University. He has published articles on German and European politics in the *American Political Science Review, Political Studies, Politische Vierteljahreschrift*, and in other journals.

JACQUES HUNTZINGER is Professor of International Relations at the University of Besançon, France, He is also Associate Professor of Strategic Studies at University of Paris I (Sorbonne). He is an expert on the French Socialist Party and international affairs. Dr. Huntzinger has published widely in the area of international problems. His articles have appeared in *Politique Etrangerie*, *Europe Archiv*, *Le Monde*, *Nouvelle Revue Socialiste*. Dr. Huntzinger holds a doctoral d'Etat of public law from the University of Paris and a political science diploma from the Institut d'Étude Politiques de Paris.

JOHN ROPER is the Labour Member of Parliament for the Farnworth constituency. Until 1970 he taught in the Faculty of Economics at the University of Manchester. Since entering the House of Commons he has taken an active part in the debates on Europe and on defense, and he is now Chairman of the Labour Committee for Europe and Vice Chairman of the Parliamentary Labour Party's Defence Group. Mr. Roper has an M.A. from Oxford University and did postgraduate work on a Harkness Fellowship at the University of Chicago.

MARTIN SAETER is Director of Research at the Norwegian Institute of International Affairs in Oslo. From 1970 to 1974 he was Associate Professor at the Institute for Political Science, University of Oslo. Dr. Saeter has written several books and many articles on European integration, the German question, and East/West relations. His most recent book is *Europa politisch. Alternativen, Modelle und Motive der Integrationspolitik*, 2d ed. (revised), Berlin 1977, (1st ed. 1974). He is the coeditor of M. Saeter and I. Smart, *The Political Implications of North Sea Oil and Gas*, University Press, Oslo, and IPC Science and Technology Press, Surrey, England, 1975. Dr. Saeter holds a cand. philol. degree from the University of Oslo (1962). He was promoted to Dr. of philosophy (Poli. Sci.) in 1972 (thesis *Det politiske Europa. Europeisk integrasjon: teori, ide og praksis*, University Press, Oslo 1971).

GEORGE WINDELL is a Professor of History at the University of New Orleans. He is the author of *The Catholics and German Unity: 1866–1871* (Minneapolis: University of Minnesota Press, 1954); "Leon Blum and the Crisis Over Spain, 1936," *The Historian*, vol. XXIV (August 1962); "Hitler, National Socialism, and Richard Wagner," *Journal of Central European Affairs*, XXII (January 1963); "The Bismarckian Empire as a Federal State, 1866–1880: A Chronicle of Failure," *Central European History*, II (December 1969); and "Hegel, Feuerbach, and Wagner's *Ring*," *Central European History* IX (March 1976). Dr. Windell received his Ph.D. from the University of Minnesota.

RELATED TITLES

Published by
Praeger Special Studies

THE FRENCH COMMUNIST PARTY IN TRANSITION: PCF-CPSU Relations and the Challenge to Soviet Authority
Annette Eisenberg Stiefbold

THE PORTUGUESE REVOLUTION AND THE ARMED FORCES MOVEMENT
Rona M. Fields

TERRITORIAL POLITICS IN INDUSTRIAL NATIONS
edited by Sidney Tarrow,
Peter J. Katzenstein,
and Luigi Graziano

HOUSING IN ITALY: Urban Development and Political Change
Thomas Angotti

INDUSTRIAL POLICIES IN WESTERN EUROPE
edited by Steven J. Warnecke
and Ezra N. Suleiman